BENEATH
BRITISH SEAS

BENEATH BRITISH SEAS

ALAN JAMES

SWAN·HILL
PRESS

First published in the UK in 1997
by Swan Hill Press, an imprint of Airlife Publishing Ltd

British Library Cataloguing-in-Publication Data
   A catalogue record for this book
   is available from the British Library

ISBN 1 85310 761 1

Typeset by Phoenix Typesetting, Ilkley, West Yorkshire, England
Printed in Hong Kong

Swan Hill Press
an imprint of Airlife Publishing Ltd
101 Longden Road, Shrewsbury, SY3 9EB, England

Contents

Close details of multi-coloured
jewel anemones *Corynactis
viridis* (Hillsea Point Rocks)

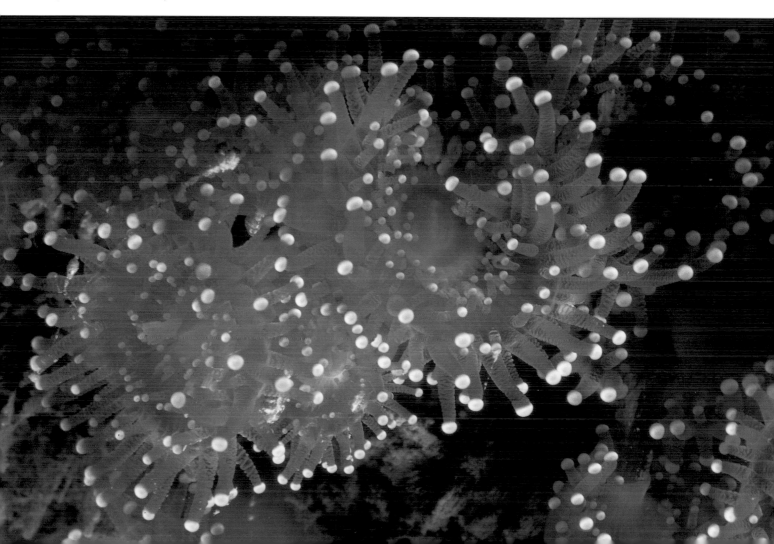

Foreword

My first sea dive was in Hartlepool dock. Not an exotic location you might think, especially as it was over thirty years ago when that particular stretch of the English coast counted among the most polluted in the world. The water in the harbour, however, was clear and I watched a large bright green rag worm making its serpentine way across the seabed in front of me. To me this was just as exciting as my first encounter with a hammerhead shark in the middle of the Indian Ocean. Why do the movies give these wonderful fish such a bad image? And why are the vast majority of films and books set in tropical waters where the giant brown seaweeds cannot grow?

East, west and home waters really are the best and here to prove it is a super book. America may have the biggest and Australia the most diverse kelp forest in the world, but a dive amongst the waving fronds of our marine algae is a never to be forgotten experience, with surprises in store around every corner. What more could anyone want than an encounter with a Farne Island grey seal, the rarest large mammal in the world! Well, it was back in the early part of this century before it was given the protection of a special Act of Parliament. For how much longer will that protection last? Already fishermen are demanding a 75 per cent cull of this friendly creature, and how much longer is it going to stay friendly if we start mass killing to save 'our' fish stocks? What arrogance!!!

It is the squabbling trawler tycoons of the world who are killing off the fishing industry by their greed. When I started diving all our harbours were full of small boats, fishing fleets that knew the limits of their local waters while providing us with fresh fish. Now most of those boats have gone and neither divers nor seals are to blame. The culprit is over-exploitation using methods that damage the resource and employ very few people.

Then there are the whales. More and more people are reporting seeing whales and dolphins in our home waters. Good news indeed! However, the Norwegian whaling industry is beginning to demand their 'fair' share in the name of sustainable development. A concept dreamed up by their prime minister, Gro Harlem Bruntland. A good idea, yes, but it is rapidly becoming the 'scam' of the century: an excuse to get their hands on everything that is left of the wild, wonderful world upon which we all depend.

One thing that gives me hope is the number of people, young and old, that are taking to the water to capture that ultimate experience: the challenge of the wilderness is waiting there just below the low tide line. The more people who learn first hand about the beauty and wonder of the biodiversity of Earth's inner space, the more people will be able to speak out in defence of that living world.

May I suggest that you sit in the bath complete with dive mask and savour the pictures in this book. Then take to the waters, our waters, and see it all for yourselves and do all in your power to help forward the cause of conservation by joining the Marine Conservation Society of which I am proud to be a founder member.

David Bellamy

Introduction

During the beautiful warm summer of 1995, British diving was probably at its best for many years. The middle of August saw me in a RIB completing a memorable trip across the English Channel towards St Helier on Jersey. I was enjoying being out on a calm, blue sea. This return journey completed what had been a wonderful day, diving and photographing the abundant and colourful marine life in the calm, clear waters of Sark in the Channel Islands.

I recalled the marine life encounters afforded to me during this lovely summer day, for I was once again buzzing with a warm privileged feeling, gained, as on countless previous occasions, from yet more first-class British diving! Throw in the good company of friendly local divers and I was guaranteed to return to the shore as a very happy and contented man.

Diving the area of Sark was 'the finale' to my first week of diving within the Channel Islands, during which I visited lovely shallow underwater gardens in *Les Minquiers* and dived on an exciting German minesweeper wreck in excellent visibility.

'From small observations, grow the seeds of great adventures.'

I added this caption to a few framed words that hang on my wall along with a few favoured underwater images. Jacques Cousteau wrote these words for his book *The Silent World.* David Doubilet then used them as a lead into the introduction of his first book *Light in the Sea.* They conclude:

'I put my eyes under again and civilisation vanished with one last bow, I was in a jungle never seen by those who floated on the opaque roof.'

These wonderful words, written by one of my heroes and used to great effect by another, always return me to my first small experience of life beneath the waves. During a winter holiday in 1985 at Israel's Red Sea resort of Elat, I donned flippers and face mask and decided to take a look. Civilisation certainly vanished, to be replaced by some of the colourful wonders of nature. I was immediately hooked by that experience and have remained so by many others ever since.

The years which have followed that initial introduction have all been influenced by life in the sea. I have dived in many of the lovely coral seas of the world, and cherish each and every diverse marine life encounter wherever it might be. But my home is in England. Its coast and temperate seas are now my much loved 'studio'. Here colourful marine life to equal any coral reef can become my next photographic subject.

Some of the these I might first have seen and appreciated in other underwater photographers work. It often becomes a challenge to emulate the quality of images. Given time, determination, and not just a little frustration, some of these subjects have been composed in my viewfinder and eventually successfully transferred to my film.

My UK photographic adventures include:

Unexpectedly finding the rare British sunset cup coral, which I photographed while diving on a superb 50-metre drop off the small isle of L'Etac, located just off of the south-west coast of Sark in the Channel Islands.

The thrill of photographing my first playful grey seal. It pushed its whiskery nose flat against my mask and then rolled over and grunted just like a puppy when I tickled its tummy. This encounter occurred within an hour of my first arrival on Lundy for a week of heavenly diving during a superb British summer.

Spending time photographing a colourful cuttlefish just off the shore at Shoalstone Reef near Brixham. It had just caught its lunch, a small spider crab, and was not really in the mood for uninvited guests. It went through fantastic colour changes to show its concern. But just under two hours later its tentacles were entwined with my fingers. It allowed my 15mm lens within inches of its head, and my macro probes right around its inky blue-black eye.

A shallow water springtime study of a fascinating lonely male lumpsucker, photographed during its two month commitment to protecting and cleaning the thousands of eggs of its long-gone female partners. Undeterred by storms, this slow-swimming, deep-water fish uses a large sucker on its underbelly to lock onto rock formations directly below the eggs to avoid being swept away.

Diving the marine-life encrusted and famous Scottish wreck the *Hispania*. It sits upright and intact in around 25 metres of water in the Sound of Mull. Trying to take in all of its photographic features in just one dive is impossible!

Photographing a fabulous garden of multi-coloured dahlia anemones on the rocky floors of 'Conservation Cave' in the Summer Isles during October. Large thunderous Atlantic swells that crashed against the back of the vertical cave walls above, sent constant shockwave reminders to me not to foul up on buoyancy control.

The pages of this book make no attempt to be a British dive guide, or in any way suggest that only the sites mentioned are worthy dive destinations. The British coast is full of wonderful diving opportunities. The ones highlighted are prominent diving locations that I have visited and consider to have enriched my personal experience of British diving.

What this book does attempt to show is the beauty and diversity of the marine life that still exists around the British coast, and to hopefully help English Nature and the Marine Conservation Society in their efforts to get across the important message 'that our seas should be given more care and consideration to allow nature to continue to evolve unheeded'. Thereby continuing to produce 'the wonders beneath British seas'.

CHAPTER 1
The Channel Islands

W hile studying the behaviour of a curious ballen wrasse, I was approached by a shoal of bass. Due to my relaxed and static position, they circled around me getting closer than I had ever seen them before. The sun danced on the surface of the clear blue Atlantic water just 5 metres above me. It sent down ever-changing rays of light that flashed along the shoal's metallic flanks. This was occasionally shadowed by the moving dive boat waiting above, which added a little more action to this interesting scene. I took no pictures since my films had all been exposed on a dive that was nearing its end. I was content and revelled in the lovely environment that the bass created for the completion of my dive.

James Mason explores the wreck of the *Schokland* off the south coast of Jersey

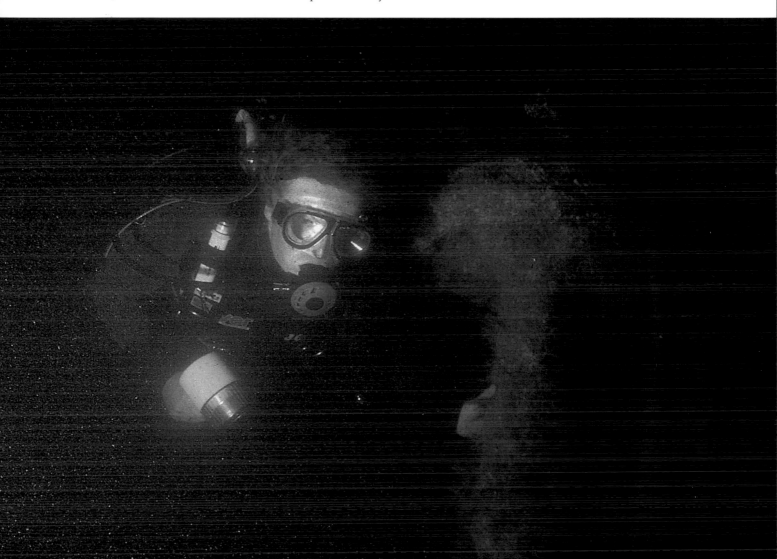

I surfaced to the smiling faces of James Nagy and his friends Alison and Jamie.

'Well what do you think,' said James.

'How long have you got,' came my reply, followed by, 'I've just been on a magical dive in "fairyland".'

Just three and a half hours earlier on a beautiful, calm summer morning, we had been loading *Surf Dive and Ski*'s spacious RIB in St Helier's deep-water harbour. Our trip across to Sark was full of expectation but we had to get the timing right. The Channel Islands have one of the highest tidal changes in the world and slack water windows are vital for safe diving in high-energy areas.

The magical dive was in fact a vertical wall on the small isle of l'Etac, situated just off the south-west coast of Sark. It came highly recommended by James with a good briefing on the marine life available. Entering the water, well armed with both macro and wide-angle cameras, I was not to be disappointed. Descending, I passed colourful subjects that were noted for attention on ascent. Levelling off at around 40 metres, I was impressed by both the visibility and high light levels that created a vista equal to that of any coral reef. Even the water temperature of 17 degrees was warm by UK standards.

My attention was demanded by the large, slow-growing orange gorgonian sea fans that grew all around. They stretched their arms across the current from the steep drop-off walls, some had their white polyps fully extended collecting

James Nagy illuminates the *Schokland* propeller

precious food. A bright yellow branching sponge *Axinellas sp*, and a red fingers, *Aleyonium glomeratum* adopted a similar stance, allowing them to capitalise on this high-energy site. The beautiful gold-coloured hydroid *Aglaeophenia plumosa*, another filter feeder, adopted prominent positions. Fill in the rock walls between these subjects with colonies of multi-coloured jewel anemones, flatworms, Devonshire cup corals and countless other macro subjects and it is confirmed that this is a highly commendable site.

Ascending this wall was pure pleasure. With both macro and wide-angle photography exposed almost at will. At around 22 metres I saw some distant 'yellow flowers' on an overshadowed wall. Was I once again on Lundy Island? No! This was a real treat, for it was a very rare colony of *Leptopsammia*, thc bright yellow and orange sunset cup corals. This beautiful and very photogenic subject was first recorded in Lundy by marine biologist Keith Hiscocks during 1969. It was, at that time, only the second recorded sighting of this subject outside of its native territory in the Mediterranean.

A resident shoal of pollack patrol the *Schokland*

A *Rhizostoma pulmo* drifting at the mercy of the prevailing current

Opposite:
A *Rhizostoma pulmo* jellyfish pulsates towards the surface sunburst

The balance of my film was completed in both wide-angle and macro cameras, forming images with both individual and groups of polyps at various stages of extension. This chance encounter accounted for an extended dive time and the relevant decompression time spent in shallow water. It also explains away my lack of frustration at having no film to capture an unusually close encounter with magnificent bass. When I eventually resurfaced I had exposed the total seventy-two images available to me, working on four of the five species of British corals at just one dive site. What did I think? 'Fairyland'.

'Fairyland' was the finale of various diving experiences during my first trip to the UK's most southerly dive destination. It had started a week earlier with a dive just a few minutes out from St Helier. The *Schokland* sank on 4/5 January 1943 with the loss of many German troops that had embarked on her. She now still sits upright and intact on the sea-bed in around 25 metres of water. My first dive on this wreck proved to be something of a challenge. Bugs in the RIB's sounding gear excluded easy wreck location. James spent a hard working and frustrating 45 minutes locating it. During this time our prime slack water period had drifted away. 'It's beginning to pull a bit,' said James with a knowing look on his face. But all six experienced divers on board decided to give it a go.

Opposite:
A fine garden of seaweeds in *Les Minquiers*

James Nagy near bollards on the bows of the M343

James Nagy astride the M343's 105mm stern gun

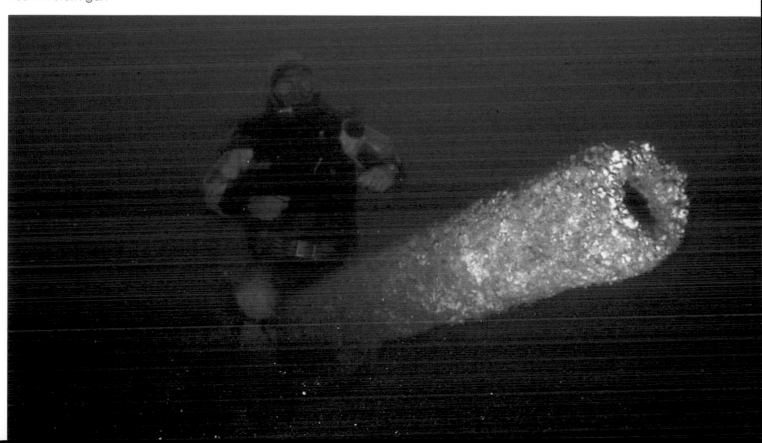

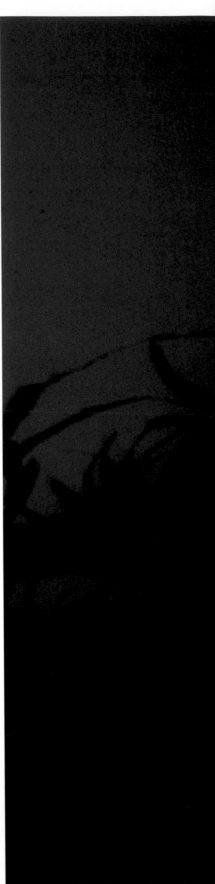

Jamie and I entered the water first, I did not fancy being last down the line. With one hand clutching cameras, the next 15 minutes were spent playing single handed 'tug-of-war' with my first introduction to Jersey's famous tides. I won! My prize was to photograph the shoals of large pollack that always abound on this wreck. The grace with which they coped with the current made me feel very clumsy indeed. I took images of Jamie hanging on to the wreck. He did not look too happy, but signalled OK. Later I was to hear that a one-week-old birthday present, a very nice divers watch, had been unknowingly lost in the battle down the line.

Our ascent was a lot easier, but not without event. We followed the buoy line from the forward port handrail at 18 metres, sliding with the current up to the buoy at the surface. Wrong! The buoy was now at 22 metres, dragged down by the current. Unimpressed, Jamie shrugged his shoulders and held out his hand. Accepting it, we flew off the line to become one with the flow. At 1,200 metres from the wreck we surfaced to a grin from James and the repeated comment 'It's beginning to pull a bit.'

The wreck of the German minesweeper M343 lies split in two sections in approximately 35 metres of water some 9 miles south-west of St Helier. It might be a little dark for good photography, but the horizontal visibility is often excellent. James followed me down the shot line located nearer the stern section. Given time to adjust, our eyes could just pick out the form of the bows in the clear, dark water. I recorded images of James exploring this wreck. He passed through a gully formed by unusual boilers approaching the bows and created an inter-esting picture near some bollards on the forecastle. Water stung my eyes as I laughed when he quickly removed his head from a gap in the deck. He was followed by the head of a huge conger eel.

Above left:
A conger eel *Conger conger* peers out from under the M343 deck plates

Above:
A redfinger scenic *Alcyonium glomeratum* on a
south-facing wall of l'Etac

The good visibility but poor light levels around this wreck prompted me to try my hand at a few time exposures to increase the amount of detail that might be recorded, but I still fired my undedicated strobe unit to enhance foreground details. I used one piece of wreckage as a tripod to photograph another, and was quite pleased with some of the results. I even tried a shot of James (normally an ever-moving target) when he found and sat astride the barrel of a large gun mounted on the deck. But I was unable to convey to him why I needed him to keep still. If only just for a few moments!

Above:
A gorgonian seafan *Eunicella verrucosa* on a south-facing wall of l' Etac

Opposite:
Redfingers *Alcyonium glomeratum* seen with polyps both extended and closed (l'Etac)

Below:
Axinella polypoides, a lovely branching sponge seen in close detail (l'Etac)

We dived other more distant sites like *Les Minquiers*, a group of small islands and reefs 10 miles to the south of St Helier. During a shallow dive in depths of no more than 10 metres and good visibility, the multitude of seaweeds and algae took on the look of an underwater garden, with colours enhanced by bright sunlight penetration.

The reflective glint of mother-of-pearl then caught my eye. It was the shell recently vacated by an 'abalone', a subject that was long gone from more accessible locations due to the common problem of over-fishing. Intrigue became a search for signs of shells that were live, for this was another subject absent from my expanding portfolio of British marine life. It was forty-five minutes later, with my eyes down to hunt, that a sudden encounter with a large swimming stingray really made me jump. Turning back towards the shelter of the rocks as the current picked up, I saw my one and only live abalone. Its green mantle was extended to graze on a crevice of rock. Delighted with this find, I battled for a pleasing image on a subject that proved awkward and time consuming to work.

A seafan *Eunicella verrucosa* close up (l'Etac)

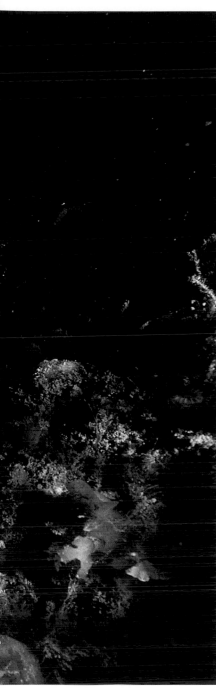

Above right:
Aglaeophenia plumosa make a
fine golden display (l'Etac)

The yellow sponge *Polymastia
boletiforme* (l'Etac)

My air supply was now depleted from my long shallow dive, which demanded that I surface prior to completing my latest roll of film. But above in the sunburst, a final subject appeared. It was the large *Rhizostoma pulmo* jellyfish drifting in the ever-increasing flow. I worked with it right to the surface. Here a hand grabbed my camera and someone said 'Alan, we really do have to go!'

Close details of a sunset coral
Leptopsammia (l'Etac)

CHAPTER 2
The Scilly Islands

My partner Julie and I sat on a small mount above the lifeboat station at Hugh Town. We were enjoying the last rays of the sun as it crashed towards the western horizon that was the Atlantic Ocean. The peninsula of rock that formed the garrison and Porth Cressa transformed into a silhouette, as did all the small craft anchored within St Mary's pool. My eyes scanned the vista from west to east, taking in St Agnes and the Western Rocks close to the south-west channel. Looking north, the close-knit islands of Samson, Bryher, and Tresco still glowed in the rays of the sun. To the east stood St Martin's with the Eastern Isles completing the scene. It was good to sit here enjoying a very relaxed end to what had been an action-packed day.

We had awoken early that morning to a fine Cornish sunrise. Thoughts of forth-coming adventures immediately took sleep from my mind. Just two hours later we were heading for the Scillies in a low-flying helicopter that allowing dramatic views of Cornwall and the south-western approaches. Julie had laughed when writing our luggage labels, 'Destination: The Scilly Islands, Accommodation: Nowhere'. Perhaps to be followed by 'Reason for visit: The mad hatter's tea party'.

Twenty minutes later saw us touching down in St Mary's. The local bus driver did not turn a hair when we asked the fare to 'Nowhere'.

On our arrival at about 9 am, we were met by Olive Fiddler, a Bristol Underwater Photography Group member who was already in residence. She introduced me to Mark Groves, dive boat skipper and keen underwater photo-grapher, and, of course, responsible for owning this place called 'Nowhere'.

The conversation went something like this.

'Hello Mark, I'm pleased to meet you! Can I introduce you to my partner Julie.'

'Hi! The dive boat leaves at 9.15, no rush!' This was followed by a wry grin at all the excess of luggage around me and then he was gone.

Message received. I kitted up in the garden, grabbing cameras and film as I went. Julie asked, 'What about our accommodation?' 'I'll take a look at it later,' came my reply. This was followed by another wry grin at all the excess of luggage around her and then I was gone.

This small group of islands lie approximately 30 miles south-west of Land's End. The sandy channels that run between them are shallow. Occasional low Autumn spring tides still allow a known sandy walk through the group, which were, not long ago, in geographical terms all one island (except, perhaps, for St Agnes). They form the western end of a granite mass that creates much of the mainland of Cornwall and continues into the tors of Dartmoor. The seas outside the channel quickly become deep, perhaps giving false security to many ships that have become wrecks. Add to these wrecks some deep granite walls and dramatic pinnacles and archways covered in some of the UK's most prolific marine life, throw in the odd encounter with grey seals and you have the recipe for some great Scillies diving!

Fully extended and feeding plumerose anemones *Metridium senile* (Western Rocks)

A ballen wrasse *Labrus bergylta* tends the anemone 'gardens' of the Western Rocks

A fast-moving, seven-armed starfish *Luidia ciliaris* feels its way through colonies of jewel anemones (Western Rocks)

Close focus *Sagartia elegans* (Western Rocks)

I descended a 100-foot vertical granite wall at Trenemene, part of the western rocks. It was a complete mass of colonies of different coloured plumerose anemones. The reef was topped off by long, well-spaced kelp fronds that completed synchronised displays in the swell and spectacular rockeries of *Sagartia elegans* spread everywhere under this 'dance'. The gardens were cared for by large ballen wrasse that continuously tended the scene. It was probably the finest show of static marine life I had ever seen. It was sustained by the rock's position in the mainstream of the Atlantic tidal flow, which brought these filter feeders a continual supply of suspended food.

Engine blocks of shipwrecks rarely capture a photographer's eye. Try diving the wreck of the *Brinkburn* to photograph a different scene. The *Brinkburn* was a London registered ship of some 3,229 tons gross. It was returning from America with a cargo of cotton and cotton seed meal when it fell foul of Maiden Bower Rocks during thick fog and sank on the 15/16 December 1898. The superstructure

Dense colonies of pink jewel anemones *Corycactis viridis* adorn the canyon walls at Hard Lewis Rock

The bright yellow sponge *Polymastia boletiforme* (Old Town, Gilstone)

Feeding redfingers *Alcyonium glomeratum* (Old Town, Gilstone)

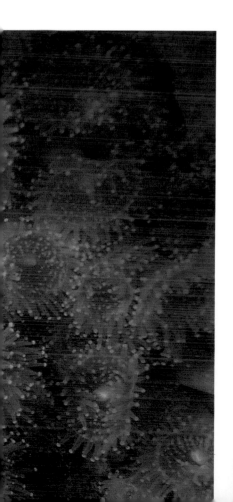

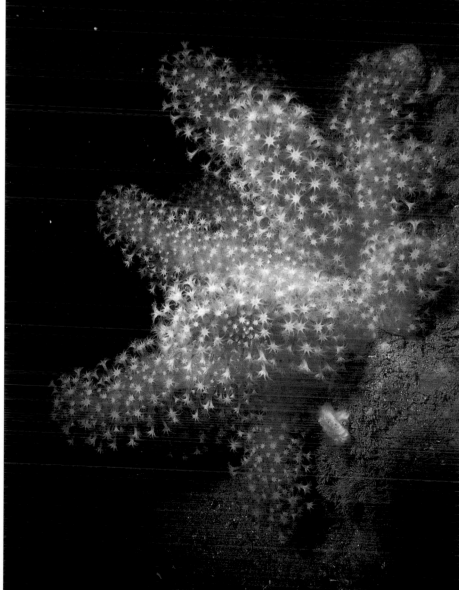

The *Brinkburn* engine block/propshaft coupling

A grey seal within inches of a wide-angle lens (Eastern Isles)

and hull of this ship have long since been dismantled, torn apart by the ravages of many Atlantic storms, but somehow the prominent engine components have survived and now sit upright on a 15-metre reef. Bringing in a diver and a sunburst creates an incredible wide-angle scene. Extending from the engine is a coupling joined to the ship's propshaft. The shaft is suspended in places and can be used to create some interesting angles. At the end of this shaft in 30 metres is a disappointedly battered old propeller. While inspecting it I caught sight of a 4-foot long bull huss, the first that I had ever seen. I took shots as it hid in the deck plates. But then wanting to improve on composition with full images I chanced tickling its tail from behind. It was in no mood to co-operate and so departed, swimming slowly and gracefully away in its undulating shark-like manner, leaving me to contemplate what might have been.

On a lovely dive at Hard Lewis Rock in the Eastern Isles, I dived along valley walls covered in jewel anemones reflecting the sun. On the valley floor a huge ancient anchor, probably weighing several tons, was propped against the side wall as if on display outside of *The Mermaid* public house near Hugh Town harbour. Drifting on, I passed effortlessly through long boulder canyons that were decorated with soft corals and sponge. As I surfaced I had to take care with the many jellyfish all around. Eventually the gaping twin hulls of Mark's hard boat with its unique central divers hatch came to engulf me. It felt like being prey to a large predator or perhaps a helpless victim in a 'James Bond' movie.

It would be sacrilege to visit the Scillies without trying your luck with the grey seals on the Eastern Isles. We entered a bay where nine grey seals were hauled out. Joe Foxcroft, another Bristol Underwater Photography Group member, slipped over the side in less than 4 metres of water. I had worked with grey seals before, but still really enjoyed the opportunity and challenge of either trying to get close to shy seals or getting far enough away from playful ones to capture some successful images. Perhaps an added bonus from this dive was the elation with which Joe exited the water after long and close encounters. I had no difficulty relating to his enthusiasm following his first experience with these mammals that have so skilfully adapted to life in the sea. Some are so full of fun and extrude the same enthusiasm as Joe did during these wonderful encounters, while providing an excellent conclusion to diving within the Scilly Islands.

Below right:
A large unco-operative bull huss watches from the safety of mangled wreckage

Below:
A curious grey seal moves in for a closer inspection (Eastern Isles)

CHAPTER 3
The Manacles

Picture this! Sipping a long cool sloe gin while looking out over a calm blue sea, recalling the colourful reefs that had earlier enhanced your day. Monkeys, goats and little black pigs are busy all around. A little earlier you sat at a large bamboo table guarded by a pair of long, slim, antique oriental brass cannons as you dined on aubergines, rice and a spicy curry served from within half a fresh, ice-white coconut. Are you lounging on some distant exotic shore? No! You are in 'Ansalmi' land. A privileged little place!

'Ansalmi' land is perhaps better known amongst the diving fraternity as Porthkerris Land and Sea Sports Centre. It is located on the east side of the Lizard Peninsula in Cornwall. To me it remains exotic. The above scenario is fact and relates to my experience of the tropical ambience of the large sunlit restaurant area adjoining the dive shop. Another good reason would be the hospitality that the 'Ansalmi families' have extended to me and my buddies during various dive trips here. Yet another reason might be that the famous Manacles Reef lies just ten minutes out from Porthkerris Beach.

The Manacles are famous for both their scenic reefs and the many ships that have come to grief on them, creating wrecks that now lie scattered in depths between 5 and 60 metres. Perhaps the most famous of these wrecks is the *Mohegan* – a 6,500 ton passenger liner that ended its days here on 14 October 1898 with the loss of 106 lives. Seen off-course and dangerously close to the reefs by the Manacle Point coastguard, a warning flare was fired and the *Mohegan* responded turning out for clearer and deeper waters. But its fate was sealed when it fouled the shallow underwater pinnacle of Vase Rock with the resulting loss of its rudder. Unable to dictate any further headway, it was destined to be wrecked on the reefs.

A ballen wrasse *Labrus bergylta* patrolling its territory on Vase Rock

A fine female cuckoo wrasse *Labrus mixtus* in her territory under the rudder shaft

I dived on the *Mohegan*, which now lies broken with her boilers and stern in approximately 20 metres of water. The main feature for me was the number of large gorgonian sea fans that dominated various vantage points across the prevailing tides. On surfacing, intrigued by the fate that had caused this wreck, I turned to Gary Fox, a wily northerner whose wit was as sharp as his diving experience. He is senior diving instructor at Porthkerris.

I asked, 'Do you know the location of the *Mohegan*'s rudder.'

Gary wasted little conversation, but grinned, 'Why?'

I followed, 'I would love a chance to dive on it.'

Gary replied, 'Well you just wait until we've been back for lunch!'

I pushed my luck a little harder. Gary was an accomplished underwater photographer with some expensive wide-angle and dual-strobe equipment. This would make a lovely photographer prop. But he was one of the most reluctant I had ever seen. I said, 'How about bringing along your camera!' Giving me a wide-eyed look, he powered the boat off to shore.

A spiny starfish scavenges on the rudder of the *Mohegan*

A few hours later I rolled backwards and entered the water. Descending down on to the shallow pinnacle of Vase Rock. As I waited for my 'guide' I took scenic shots of kelp on granite rocks covered in static marine life, with bright coloured ballen wrasse patrolling around. I was then treated to the sight of Gary, complete with his camera and strobes. He seemed to take on the roll of a huge 'preying mantis', so I decided to stay out of reach. He gave me a signal to follow and disappeared through an anemone-covered gully and on down over the reef. Within minutes he had located the *Mohegan*'s rudder, spreading his hands out wide in a gesture that said 'easy', he waved and moved on a little farther on.

There before me on the reef, in all its innocence and beauty, lay the approximately 25-foot steel rudder that caused the cruel fate of the *Mohegan*. It now lies with its raggedly sheared solid main stock dramatically suspended over large granite boulders. Nature has since been to work on this piece of history, turning both this stock and the whole rudder into a colourful memorial garden in honour of all those who lost their lives when it sank nearly one hundred years ago.

Actinothoe sphyrodeta fully extended as tentacles transfer food to its mouth (*Mohegan* rudder)

Close details of colonial pink jewel anenomes *Corynactis viridis* (*Mohegan* rudder)

Below right:
A male cuckoo wrasse *Labrus mixtus* patrols the top of Raglan Reef

Kelp fronds grow only from the top of the broken stock, the rest of the rudder is home to multitudes of multi-coloured *Sagartia elegans* and colonies of jewel anemones creating a photographer's macro dream. A colourful territorial orange female cuckoo wrasse had taken up residence under the stock. The rudder is tended by two of the seas cleaners, the sea urchin and their distant cousin, the bright spiny starfish.

I finally ascended a shot line towards the surface from this dive on which I had spent quite some time. The pull of the strong current that creates the abundant marine life I had just experienced was now making it difficult to ascend the line while taking care of precious cameras. I was tired by the time I eventually left the water. Gary took advantage saying, 'Was that all right then!' It was fine, but all I could do was give him a look and a just nod. But he had not finished 'Where would you like to go now then.' Saving conversation I just gasped, 'Home'.

The next day we were joined by a group of divers from a Poole BSAC. We all agreed that we would like to dive on the very scenic Raglan Reef. Not being a technical diver, and not having a lot of excess diving kit, I was attracted by the photographic potential of the array of equipment donned by these helmeted, mixed-gas divers prior to diving. One unknown lady agreed to buddy me during this dive.

Below left:
Diver interaction with an inquisitive female cuckoo wrasse near the top of Raglan Reef

Below:
An ever-searching spiny starfish amid colonies of jewel anemones on Raglan Reef

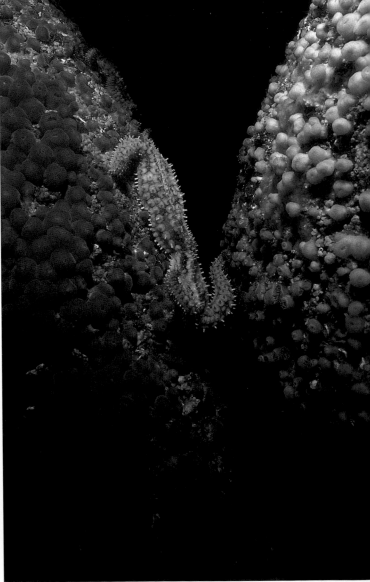

A feeding gorgonian sea fan *Eunicella verrucosa* spreads across the prevailing current collecting food (Wreck of the *Mohegan*)

Close details of feeding red-fingers *Alcyonium glomeratum* (Raglan Reef)

Raglan Reef is another granite pinnacle that ascends from around 40 metres to within 2 metres of the surface. Kelp-topped, its shallow, high-energy areas are a mass of orange through to white dead mens' fingers, with plumerose anemones also competing for space. As we descended the 'twin headlights' of my buddy lit up this scene and added more than a little drama to some of my shots. I worked on spiny starfish in crevices covered with different coloured colonies of jewel anemones, going in very close for compositional effect. In deeper water a fine example of dead mens' fingers in very subtle hues demanded some attention. Large gorgonian sea fans and small colonies of orange light bulb tunicates also called for film. As we ascended towards the surface and the completion of this dive, my buddy created an amusing scene. An inquisitive female cuckoo wrasse became convinced that the holes in a poorly maintained glove were in fact food, not exposed fingers. It seemed determined that we should not leave until they were eaten. This situation took care of my last few frames, leaving me a little more satisfied than the wrasse, which we left to its own devices, feeling assured that the wealth of life on the Manacles would no doubt soon provide!

Below left:
A colony of orange sea-squirts
Clavelina sp (Raglan Reef)

Below:
A small Bloody Henry starfish crosses large boulders on Raglan Reef

CHAPTER 4
The Falmouth Area

During August I spent a few days diving an area somewhat different to many of the reefs and pinnacles that I often visit. Andrew Sawyer Parker and Gordon James, two prominent members of the Bristol Underwater Photography Group, invited me to join them and experience diving both within the Fal estuary, and the immediate seas into which it flows.

The lovely coastline of Falmouth and the Carrick Roads is famous for its natural deep-water harbour. It is reputed to be the third deepest in the world and for this reason it is steeped in naval history going way back into distant times. The sea-bed around this area must conceal the answer to a marine archaeologist's dreams. Falmouth itself came into being in the mid seventeenth century. With the name change of a place called Smithick, locally known as 'Pennycomequick'. Its deep-water channels and good location as a 'first and last port of call' assured its status as a port right into current times.

For our self-contained venture, we found a local air supply, small hotel and slipway all within easy reach. Thus saving precious moments at this busy time of the year to be spent diving from Gordon's well-equipped little boat, which, for reasons unknown to me at that time, was unflatteringly named *The Grey Pig.*

Our first dive took us east across the Fal estuary. We headed to within a few hundred yards of the shore just north of St Mawes Castle. It was built by order of Henry VIII in the early sixteenth century. The sea-bed below this picturesque setting was not by my experience 'full of historic artefacts', but it contained a fine example of British 'mearl beds' and the life that exists within them.

A blue-eyed anglerfish on the edge of the mearl beds (The Fal estuary)

Mearl consists of crunchy branching and loosely assembled particles with a colourful living outer layer. Its loose assembly supplies protective areas where many other plants and animals take up residence. It is mainly found on south and west-facing current-swept coasts that afford protection from waves.

During our long dive we drifted with the benefit of boat cover and SMBs. The landward current we entered was well under half a knot and presented no problem to a determined photographer working with delicate macro subjects. Later Andrew and I cut across an ever-increasing current, heading into deeper water of between 15 and 20 metres. We suddenly came across one, two, and then dozens of examples of *Pleurobranchus membranaceus* – a large, sporadic, sometimes free-swimming (upside down) mollusca that is capable of secreting sulphuric acid if attacked. They were breeding on the sea-bed all around. This wonderful photo opportunity was also a subject that neither of us had previously encountered.

A single carpet anemone showing pursed tentacle details (The Fal estuary)

A colony of carpet anemones covering an area near the mearl beds (The Fal estuary)

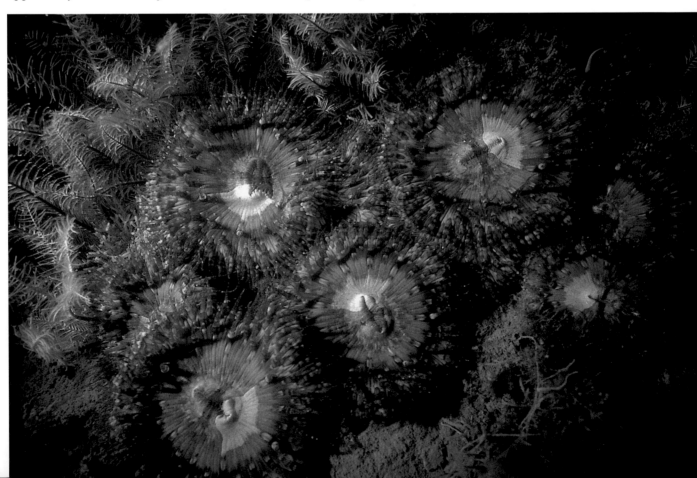

Andrew Sawyer Parker finds a large thornback ray *Raja clavata* off St Anthony Head

A large *Pleurobranchus membranaceus*, one of a sporadic group found mating and egg-laying on the mearl beds in the Fal estuary

The irony of this situation was in the fact that we were now in a current approaching 2 knots on a featureless flat bottom. All the enthusiastic finning we could muster would not sustain us in a fixed position for long enough to gain any well-composed images. Frustrated, we looked at each other and both signalled 'thumbs up' and headed for the surface feeling more than a little cheated.

Discussing this situation with Gordon, a knowledgeable marine biologist and therefore also keen to take advantage of this sighting, we all agreed to repeat dive this area before leaving Falmouth, first seeking more local information on slack water patterns in the Fal. The afternoon saw us turning left around St Anthony Head and on passed the prominent lighthouse. It was *en route* that I became educated in the interpretation of the apt naming of Gordon's little boat. It did not slice through the waves as expected, but like all little grey pigs 'it just wallowed in the troughs'.

We dived an area of shingled bottom, successfully looking for promised thornback rays. During my dive and encounters with six mature fish, I was surprised how much you needed to 'get your eye in' in order to locate such large, well camouflaged subjects. I swam right over the top of my first ray at a distance of just 2 feet. It was only the movement of its pebble-like eyes watching me that finally gave it away. Graded back mottling totally breaks up their form against the pebble-dashed sea-bed. By this and their low relief, nature has created yet another challenging subject to capture on film.

Day two saw some fine summer weather, which tempted us back out to the area dived with the rays. While previously looking for them I had also seen many of the flatfish that form part of its diet. Intrigued by the plaice and its face, I decided to compile a little photographic study of its forms. On approach, some fish would be gone at the moment of detection. Others would just act as if dead. So, being quick-thinking, I decided to work with the 'dead' ones!

Opposite:
A plaice *Pleuronectes platessa* face portrait

A large plaice *Pleuronectes platessa* lying amongst kelp fronds off St Anthony Head

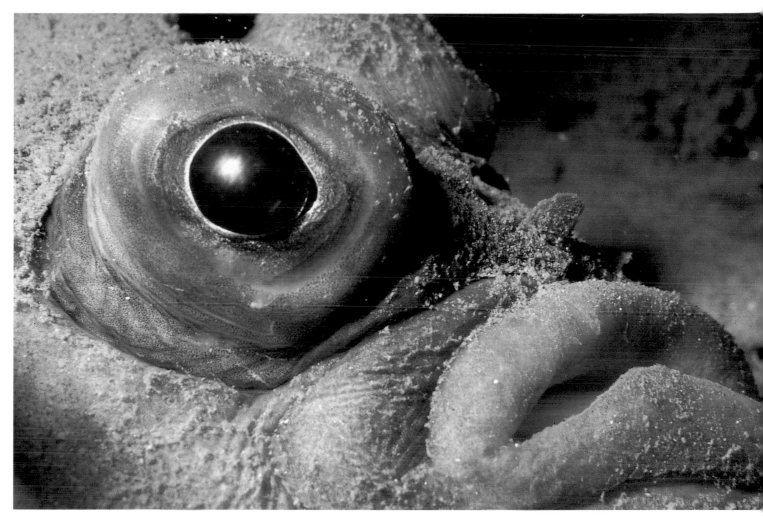

Details of plaice skin structure
Pleuronectes platessa

Later that day, while diving amid seaweeds and rocks, I was soon attracted by the fine white lines 'painted' from tentacles to tail on an otherwise subtle blue coloured *Coryphella lineata* nudibranch. I also came across a cagey little topnot. It allowed one shot, then it was gone. It flew off its rock onto the sea-bed, disturbing a scallop that took off in fright. Now a diver might pick up some scallops thinking 'supper later tonight' but for me I had just seen a little beauty, its exposed mantle colours lit by my torchlight.

On our last morning we all worked closely with the *Pleurobranchus*, with slack water aiding our quest. Long ago I thankfully adopted the practice of always have an additional wide-angle or macro camera with me, depending on what other lens I plan to work with. The reason is simply to allow more potential subject coverage as it is impossible to always predict your next subject. An example of this happened towards the end of the dive. With my macro film completed, Andrew and I headed back in the shallower water where the mearl beds give way to shallow reefs and it was there we had an exciting encounter with a superb blue-eyed anglerfish.

Close portrait of a small topnot *Zeugopterus punctatus* off St Anthony Head

Pleurobranchus membranaceus egg mass

Close up of a disturbed scallop *Pecten maximus* off St Anthony Head

A *Coryphella lineata* nudibranch meanders across the sea-bed off St Anthony Head

CHAPTER 5
Plymouth Sound

I was enjoying photographing a lovely little cowery. It passed through some feather stars, which presented it with a difficult route, but made a pleasing composition for me. Its tentacles and syphon seemed to feel the way rather than using sight from its tiny black eyes. A curious ballen wrasse joined me, constantly surveyed this scene, and seemed convinced that my lovely little subject was food! He distracted my attentions by swimming within my chosen frame area. Indeed, he was becoming a pest. By this time the cowery was losing my total attention, so, working on the principle 'if you can't beat them, photograph them', the wrasse became my subject.

Changing my macro camera for one with wide angle, I composed and exposed my first shot expecting to see the usual instant flash of light picking out the colours of the fish before fading. Nothing! I checked my flash leads, fired again and still nothing. I reverted my strobe back to my macro camera and it fired. At this stage I was fearing the worst. I looked through the port of my 15mm lens for water that I did not want to see, but it looked fine. I turned the camera upside down, looked through the viewfinder and waited. Two horrible little drops of water formed within and splashed into the top of the viewfinder.

Close details of multi-coloured jewel anemones *Corynactis viridis* (Hillsea Point Rocks)

The experience of flooding an underwater camera is certainly not new to me and it will surely happen again. It tends to stimulate an immediate desire to be anywhere but under the water. Indeed, I often humorously recall an incident in Weasel Lock in Eyemouth. A dive buddy of mine seriously flooded his precious housed Nikon F3. Following which, he surfaced with the velocity of a Polaris missile, conducted the best impression of JC walking on water that I have ever seen and, fully kitted, scaled the cliffs on to dry land, all in a matter of seconds.

Experience teaches you some sort of procedure that slows down this chain of reactions. So, I turned the sick Nik V on to its back to keep the ingress of water away from the lens. I had not a fitted battery, I rarely do, so all the electronics were safe. I comforted myself that I was shore diving in front of the very well equipped Fort Bovisand Dive Centre, so I knew that all I might need was to hand. Once ashore I set about cleaning 'sick Nik'. Ironically, I had made this early shore dive 'filling in time' while Peter Sieniewicz kindly arranged a few days of special photographic boat dives for me. I now discover that the first of these will be departing in under two hours! I recalled the last verse of a poem *The Underwater Photographer* that I once wrote. The words went some thing like this:

> There is no situation, leaves me more weak,
> And with that the feeling, I'm up the creek,
> My equipment is serviced, and looking so chic
> But my camera is flooded, I've got a leak!

During countdown the air was full of the familiar sound of hair dryers, and not just a few curses, as the components of my camera flew around. Eventually just ten minutes late, I finally arrived at the boat to be greeted by an ever-smiling John Souness, who said, 'You're not usually late.' I grinned and replied, 'I was breaking my neck for 'a leak'.'

A female ballen wrasse *Labrus bergylta* over cord-weed and kelp in Polhawn Cove

If you yearn for good company and good diving, you could do far worse than being in a dive boat with John Souness on Hillsea Point Rocks. John, a life-long Cornish diver, has an enthusiasm for diving and photography that is as long as his lively conversation, which in turn is charming, witty and endless. Hillsea Point Rocks are reputed to be the best scenic dive on this section of coast. They are in fact a group of perhaps eight pinnacles that rise to within 2 metres of the surface from the sea-bed in 26 metres.

Given the good visibility that often exists here, and having taken care to wait for slack water, John and I entered the water. These pinnacles create an exciting vista to dive, their sheer sides and the sand-filled canyons between are full of dramatic static marine life and colourful fish. I took scenic and macro images of jewel anemones near the surface. This I followed with planned shots of John descending through the kelp to achieve some close, wide-angle images of his photogenic Ikelite housing. The air trap within the transparent Lexan case creates a pleasing enhanced effect.

More time was spent with the ever present territorial male and female cuckoo wrasse, during which I marvelled at the difference between their bright colours. I took images of dead mens' fingers showing various subtle colours and hues and velvet swimming crabs hugged them looking for protection whenever I moved in close. I finally settled on a lovely Bloody Henry, watching and photographing its movement between two pure white dead mens' fingers. I used my strobes spotting light to illuminate these contrasting subjects, moving it through various angles to gain good effect. Perhaps 20 minutes later I felt something at my shoulder. It was John with large shining eyes. He gave my subject a nod of approval, and me the signal 'time to go up'.

The undulating arms of a spiny starfish *Marthasterias glacialis* feel their way across Hillsea Point Rocks

A velvet swimming crab *Liocarinus puber* seeks protection under dead mens' fingers

A vivid Bloody Henry starfish *Henricia oculata* feels its way between dead mens' fingers *Alcyonium digittum* at the bottom of Hillsea Point Rocks

A colourful male cuckoo wrasse *Labrus mixtus* moves over a reef adorned with dead mens' fingers at Hillsea Point Rocks

An elephant's ear sponge *Pachymastisma sp* on a vertical wall south of the Mewstones

A close up of the feeding white polyps of redfingers *Alcyonium glomeratum* on the Mewstones

The following day Peter had arranged another treat for me. I was joined by Fort Bovisand's well-known underwater photographer, Dave Peake. David and John have been snorkelling, diving and photographing together in Plymouth Sound for over thirty years. So I relaxed, knowing that I was once again in good hands.

Dave asked in his curt humour 'Well, what do you want?'

'I would like some ross coral, an elephant's ear sponge, and a dogfish or two, oh, and perhaps a tolerant conger eel!' I replied.

'Good god, man,' said David looking skyward. He shook his head but eventually smiled and said, 'Lets go.' I laughed at his face and did not think to ask 'Where?'

I picked my way through ross corals, a little spoilt for choice. Some of these bright orange undulating filter feeders were over two feet across. Selection finally

A noble dogfish *Scyliorhinus canicula* lying on shingle facing into the prevailing current (The Mewstones)

settled me down on a small vibrant subject. It was in an elevated location that enabled me to see some contrasting dark water behind it. This was followed by a spiny starfish and an elephant's ear sponge. Suddenly David was beckoning me to his location. Proudly sitting on clean, current-swept shingle was a lovely spotted dogfish – a subject so often seen hanging grotesquely from a fisherman's hook. It was a pleasure to see one so healthy. I circled around to approach it head on, taking images as I moved in, using careful side lighting angles for effect.

Close up of a fine example of redfingers *Alcyonium glomeratum* on the Mewstones

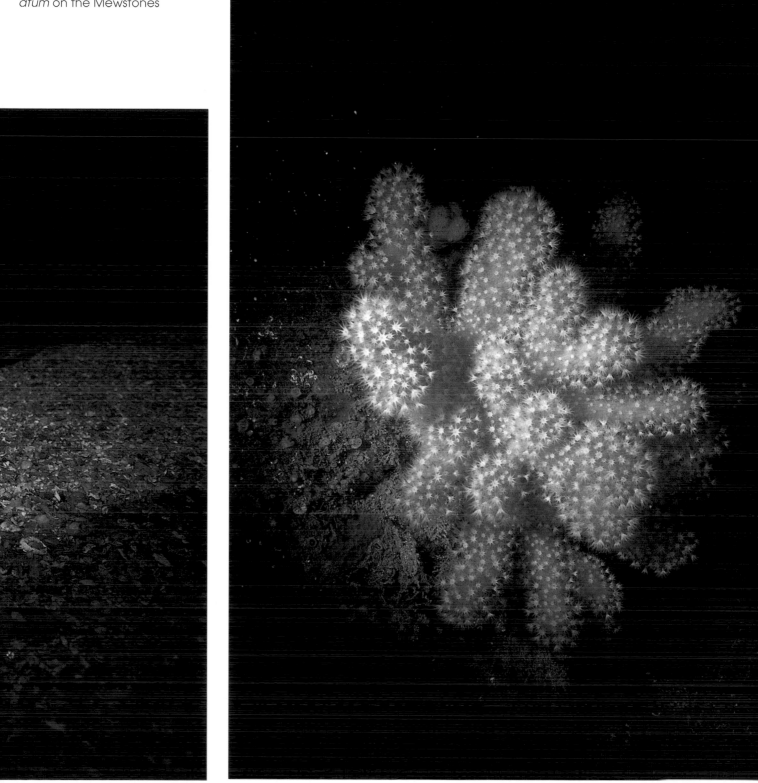

51

When back on the boat, Dave and I both smiled at each other in mutual approval. But there was one thing left on my list! Dave read my mind saying, 'If you want a guaranteed conger, I know where there is one at Polhawn Cove, but we will have to go in to the fort for more fuel first!' I just smiled and he repeated his curt 'Good god, man,' instantly followed by 'Lets go'.

Later, I waited as agreed, on a kelp-covered rock in shallow water, casually taking images of a female wrasse. Below, by contrast, David was scurrying around like a ferret in a maze of bubble-filled gullies. This man, with a great love of marine life, zealously searched to renew old encounters. I was finally introduced to a fine, extremely blue conger eel, which had recently moved home without giving anyone notice. A very brave mature prawn, judging by the size of the conger's mouth, looked dangerously unimpressed with its new neighbour.

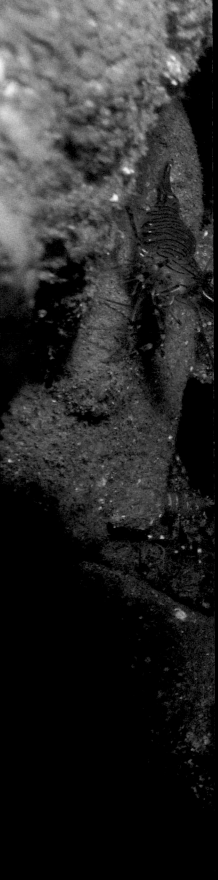

A delicate cowrie *Trivia monacha* weaves its way through feather stars *Antedon bifida* (Fort Bovisand Reef)

A lovely blue conger eel *conger conger* eyes its fearless or foolish neighbour, a common prawn, *Palaemon serratus* (Polhawn Cove)

Close detail of transparent golden light bulb tunicates, *Clavelina sp* (The Mewstones)

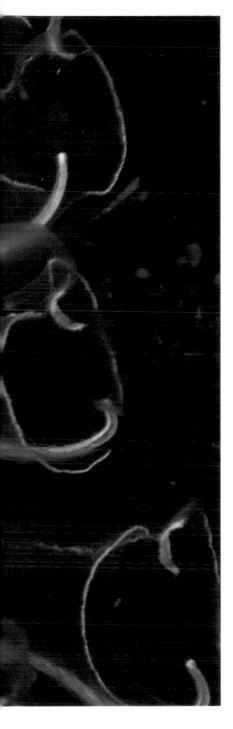

A male velvet swimming crab *Liocarcinus puber* retains a smaller female waiting for her moult to allow him to mate (Fort Bovisand Reef)

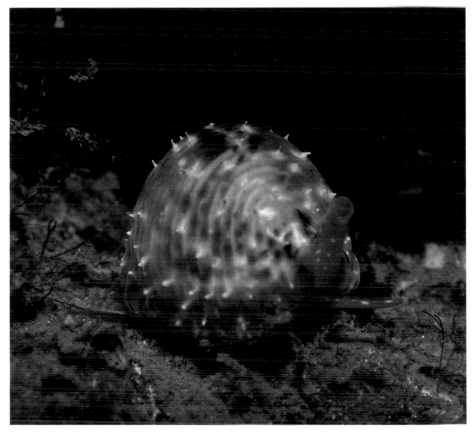

A delicate cowrie displays a full mantle *Trivia monacha* (Fort Bovisand Reef)

CHAPTER 6
The Torbay Area

Opposite:
Yellow boring sponge *Cliona celata* grow to large proportions (Shoalstone Reef)

T orbay is the closest productive coast within easy access to my home in Bristol. It is therefore an area much used, appreciated and cared about. It has, over many years, provided me with hundreds of hours of underwater photography. The subject potential is immense and my encounters include: John Dory, lumpsuckers, seals, cuttlefish, scenic caves and nudibranch, all of which have created dramatic images that stand the test of time.

Unlike most of the areas highlighted in previous chapters, Torbay is not blessed with outstanding underwater visibility, inshore this rarely exceeds five metres. It is also an area where much of the sea-bed has a fairly high silt factor. But the fact remains that marine life is abundant, even if photography is more of a challenge.

Close details of *Actinothoe sphyrodeta* (Shoalstone Reef)

Right and below right:
Lovely translucent brown and white anemones in shallow water (Shoalstone Reef)

Opposite:
A large dahlia anemone *Urticina felina* stretches its tentacles to capture prey (Shoalstone Reef)

59

This fairly difficult 'studio' has insisted that I sharpen up on my photographic procedures. In turn it makes more favourable conditions seem easy to work, with many required disciplines becoming second nature. Most of my diving in this area is shore-based in shallow water of depths rarely over 15 metres. Shore diving allows me to come and go as I please, perhaps spending two hours or more getting to know a given subject.

While kitting up in the carpark at Shoalstone Beach one morning, I watched two divers exit the water. On their approach to the carpark I said, 'The conditions look good.' A northern voice replied 'Aye, but don't bother going in, there's nowt in there.'

I sat and considered this. No, not whether to go in, but the mentality behind this broad statement. What did this guy have to see before it registered as a worthy site? Presumably sharks, shipwrecks and treasure. It seemed strange to me that someone could be so blind to endless examples of nature. Or had the English Channel suddenly become a barren sea?

A striking pink and white sponge that is prolific at Shoalstone Reef

A colony of very small white filter
feeders on a vertical rock face
(Shoalstone Reef)

I entered the water, keen to reaffirm that the sea was not dead. In just six feet of water I saw a lively shaney, a pair of feeding beadlet anemones and silhouetted kelp fronds undulating in the swell! Reassured that everything was fine, I moved on into deeper water where a group of *Actinothoe sphyrodeta* (small orange and white anemones) caught my eye. While photographing them I disturbed a small spider crab that trundled off in a huff. Smiling, I carried on working. Suddenly I was aware of a flustering movement of silt and looked around to see this luckless crab engulfed by ten colourful writhing and inescapable tentacles. A cuttlefish then extruded mucus over the crab, producing a powerful and intoxicating stupor, after which the crab's battle was lost!

Opposite:
This egg mass of the seldom seen squid was probably laid nocturnally (Shoalstone Reef)

The striking colours of a *Polycera sp* nudibranch contrasts with the kelp frond that it crosses (Shoalstone Reef)

62

Slowly approached, this cuttlefish, which was in no mood for uninvited guests, went through fantastic colour changes to show its concern and would surely have avoided this encounter if its tentacles had not been so full of crab. I moved carefully in and out, constantly testing my acceptance within its territory. Just under two hours later after gaining acceptance, its tentacles were entwined with my fingers. This cuttlefish allowed me to take wide-angle pictures within inches of its head and my macro probes were right around its inky blue-black eyes. As I finally left the water, totally thrilled by this encounter, I shook my head as I recalled that previous divers words, 'There's nowt in there!'

Opposite:
The amazingly long arms of a mud-runner crab *Goneplax rhomboides* are collapsed as it quickly returns to its burrow (Shoalstone Reef)

The cuttlefish *Sepiola sp* displays fantastic colour changes and graceful skirt movements (Shoalstone Reef)

Close details of a billowing candy-striped flatworm *Prosthecereus vittatus* as it works its way across Shoalstone Reef

64

Shoalstone is an excellent area for anemones, of which you can find dozens of species and colours in various types of terrain. In 12 to 13 metres, colonies of plumerose anemones jostle for space amongst feather stars. Nudibranchs are busy mating and laying their eggs all around and, to complete this scene, billowing candy-striped flat worms create a wonderful sight.

On a boat dive from the picturesque harbour of Paignton, I dived Black Rock, one of Torbay's many more remote reefs, and buddied with a freshly qualified young lady diver. She was full of enthusiasm for what she might see, but naturally wanted to work a close buddy system. I asked if she would model some

A diver takes a close look at one of a legion of common starfish *Aserias rubens* devouring some of Black Rock's huge colonies of common mussels *Mytilus edulus*

diver/marine life interaction for me. Proving to be an excellent diver and model she seeming quite at one with the sea. Descending Black Rock, which has an incredibly thick covering of filter-feeding black mussels, it certainly resembled its name. These mussels were under attack from legions of fat colourful common starfish, the most that I had ever seen. My buddy's eyes were unbelieving at such an incredible sight. I took a few images as she made a close inspection. We came across vertical walls and pinnacles that were in total colour contrast with the white plumerose anemones dominating the reef. She was intrigued as I photographed beautiful, delicate Devonshire cup corals and a crimson and white dahlia anemone as we reached the bottom of the reef. We watched a hermit crab feeding on fresh mussel, with a parasitic anemone sweeping up titbits of food. The crab recoiled within its whelk shell, disturbed by the flash of my strobe. This defensive action admirably displayed their symbiotic relationship, with the anemone now standing proud in defiance. The delicate red and blue hue of its tentacles stimulated the attention of my last few frames. Back on the boat I smiled as my buddy enthusiastically described her experience. She did not need sharks, shipwrecks and treasure to appreciate the wonders she had seen!

A diver examines a vertical wall of white plumerose anemones, *Metridium senile*, on Black Rock

Close up details of a single feeding plumerose anemone *Metridium senile*
(Black Rock)

A lovely Devonshire cup coral *Caryophyllia smithi* feeds from the prevailing current on Black Rock

A beautifully contrasted dahlia
anemone *Urticina felina* at the
bottom of Black Rock

A scavenging hermit crab *Pagurus bernhardus* scuttles around the sea-bed at the bottom of Black Rock

Close up portrait of a hermit crab *Pagurus bernhardus* (Black Rock)

A spider crab *Maja squinado*
mimics the above symbiosis by
having coaxed a plumerose
anemone *Metridium senile* onto
its back (Black Rock)

Opposite:
A hermit crab *Pagurus bernhardus* recoils to show the
defence symbiotic relationship
provided by a parasitic
anemone *Calliactis parasitica*
(Black Rock)

An aggressive spider crab *Maja squinado* attacks the camera, sinking a claw into my shutter finger (Black Rock)

Three spiny starfish *Marthasterias glacialis* scavenge a dead sea urchin (Black Rock)

Babbacombe Beach lies just north of Torbay, on the coast road towards Shaldon and Teignmouth. It lies at the bottom of steep cliffs, overlooked by the holiday town of Babbacombe. It is a very convenient site to dive, and has produced for me many little surprises over the years. The close proximity of these high cliffs protect this bay from much of the prevailing winds. I have dived here in a calm sea during gale force south-westerly winds. For this reason it is regularly used as a backup location when diving in this area. The Bristol Underwater Photography Group annual splash-in competition was held here in 1995 and produced quite a cross-section of subjects. I took images of Alan Mildren using his tripod to produce registered sequence images of a sunlit gully with kelp moving in the swell. John Maclarene took up the challenge by trying to get a lively tompot blenney within his framer. Kelvin Curtis entered a shallow cave system to photograph its resident large mature prawns. These translucent prawns are a fascinating and difficult subject on which to achieve good contrast, and they have such lovely colourful 'rugby socks'. Depth of field is also a problem for macro photography on a subject with so many high reliefs. But all's well, that ends well. For the Group trophy sits on my shelf.

The ever-amusing tompot blenney shown in close detail at Babbacombe

76

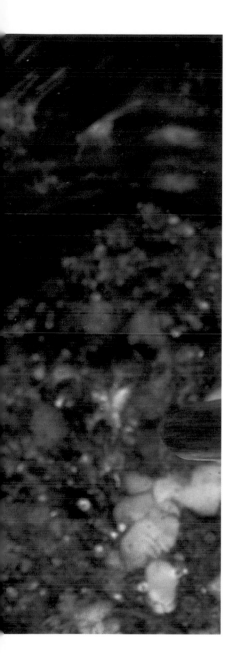

Portrait of diving photographer
Alan Mildren as he prepares to
take a sequence of kelp movements over a sunlit gully near
Babbacombe

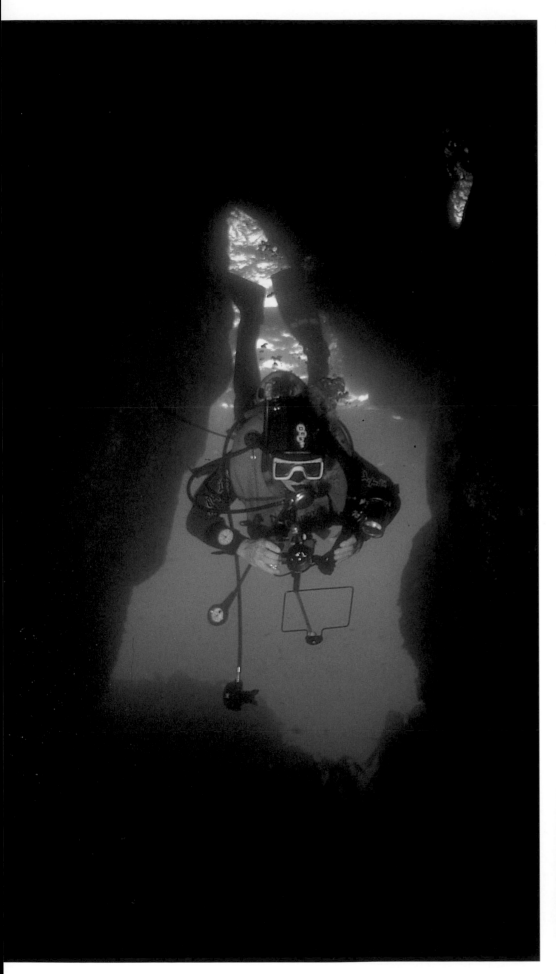

Diving photographer Kelvin Curtis enters a Babbacombe cave

A ballen wrasse *Labrus bergylta* in shallow kelp beds at Babbacombe

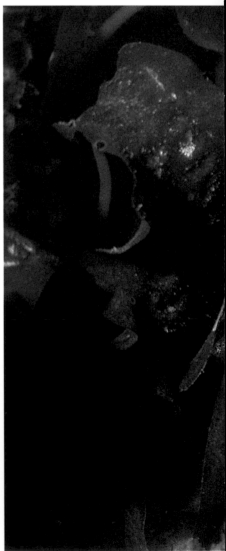

Close details of a common prawn *Palaemon serratus* (Babbacombe)

An incredible cloak anemone *Adamsia maculata* sweeps titbits from the sea-bed from its messy-eating hermit crab host *Pagurus prideauxi* (Babbacombe)

Below left:
The red and white colours of a dahlia anemone *Urticina felina* contrast a Babbacombe reef

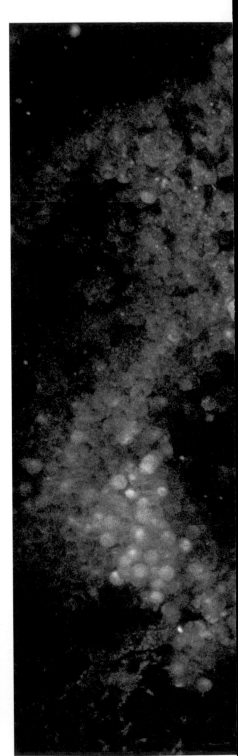

Recently I did a study of two individual male lumpsuckers protecting their eggs in this bay. These two lumpsuckers were completely different in appearance. Normally deep-water fish, they had come into shallow water to breed. Once a female has laid her eggs on an area of rock cleaned by the male she returns immediately to the deep. The luckless male is left with the task of cleaning and protecting the eggs for up to two months until they hatch.

The first of these fish had adopted a creamy white colour with liberal black speckles. This camouflaged it well into the shingled and rocky seabed area of the nest. I took images of it with its sucker locked on in front of the nest and close wide-angle images of the holes that are formed in the egg mass to allow the lumpsucker to blow clean and aerate the eggs at the back of the nest.

Below:
Close details of the male lump-sucker tending its egg mass (Babbacombe)

The second fish had its nest six feet off the bottom on the north side of an over-hanging, dark-coloured rock, its colours reflected this location making it very difficult to spot. This fish appeared to be a little more free and swam off between spats of 'blowing' on its eggs. But this behaviour turned out to be the constant repelling of a group of hungry ballen wrasse intent on eating the eggs. When it chased them away I was temporarily able to move in between the lumpsucker and the eggs to take some upward-angle, head-on shots as it returned to blow on the eggs. I marvelled at how nature had prepared this normally deep-water fish, now living in the stormy rough waters of the shallows, perhaps without eating or sleeping while protecting its eggs from all-comers during this annual two-month long obsession.

Details of the lumpsucker's egg mass showing blow holes for cleaning and oxygenating and additional cleared rock that allows the lumpsucker to lock on during rough sea conditions (Babbacombe)

A balanced lumpsucker returns to its eggs following the eviction of yet another ballen wrasse (Babbacombe)

CHAPTER 7
Chesil Beach, Portland

S een from high on Portland, Chesil Beach is an amazing geographical feature. Its huge deposits of graded pebbles curve westwards past Abbotsbury, stretching for 18 miles along the south coast. Diving in this area is often blessed with good underwater visibility of 15 metres or more.

A lionsmane jellyfish pulsates near the surface in Chesil Cove

The cove is probably the most scenic site with lots of huge Portland stone boulders providing habitats for the abundant marine life. An array of colourful seaweeds form an undergrowth where individual large pollack and wonderful John Dory hunt. Lionsmane and moon jellyfish pass by on the prevailing current and the sea-bed often reveals bright, skilfully camouflaged scorpion fish patiently waiting to catch their prey. They in turn need to be careful with lots of hungry cuttlefish around. While diving here I came across an intriguing subject that had been dead for thousands of years – it was a large partially exposed fossil at least a foot across.

In 1872 the *Royal Adelaide*, one of the original steel-hulled ships built in Bristol in 1865, was wrecked here a little to the north of Portland. It now lies on Chesil Beach in just 12 metres of water, 150 yards from the shore. During August 1991, following a dive in the cove, I heard divers discussing recent sightings of grey triggerfish on this wreck. My ears picked up immediately at the mention of this reportedly shy and, at that time, rarely seen visitor to our shores.

A diver exploring the bow section of the *Royal Adelaide*

A triggerfish *Balistes carolinesis* feeds close to the camera (The *Royal Adelaide*)

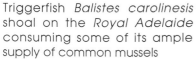
Triggerfish *Balistes carolinesis* shoal on the *Royal Adelaide* consuming some of its ample supply of common mussels

Deciding to check out these sightings, I obtained instructions on how to locate the wreck and returned a few days later armed with my usually array of photography kit. I made the short swim out to the *Royal Adelaide* full of enthusiasm to capture images of this diverse subject. Soon the only remaining intact section of this wreck, the bows, loomed up before me. To my surprise, I immediately identified a single triggerfish swimming out over the wreck. Busying myself altering camera setting so that I made less impact when moving in closer to it, I was shocked as I looked up to see the triggerfish less than a foot in front of my mask. I literally jumped at this unexpectedly close encounter but recovered my composure enough to take a few excited shots. Losing interest the fish swam back up over the bows and continued back onto the wreck. I followed being careful not to incite a chase.

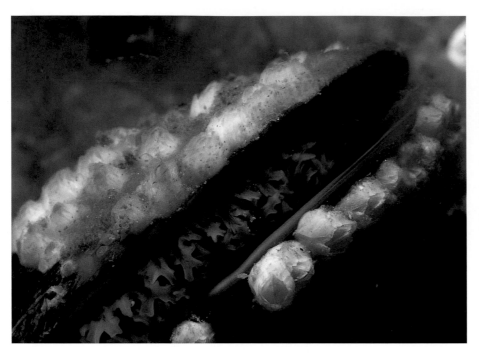

Mantle details of the common mussel *Mytilus edulus* (The *Royal Adelaide*)

A feeding cream plumerose anemone *Metridium senile* bows in the current (The *Royal Adelaide*)

A tight colony of bright red jewel anemones *Corynactis viridis* (The *Royal Adelaide*)

I was then greeted by a sight far more rewarding than I could ever have hoped for in my efforts to gain a few triggerfish shots. A shoal, fifty to sixty strong were swimming around the *Royal Adelaide*. They were feeding on the wreck's abundant mussels with their eight powerful chisel-like teeth. These fish were not shy as reported sightings had said. They were very diver-friendly, and literally swam across the wreck to meet me, creating a sight that I will never forget. I set to work trying to capture this scene, but the irregular movements of the shoal made it difficult to achieve a good composition. I was also pestered by inquisitive fish repeatedly swimming too close to my lens.

During late October that year, I returned to the *Royal Adelaide* with my buddy Alan Mildren, with the obvious intent of further triggerfish encounters. Imagine our disappointment on reaching the wreck to find that all the triggerfish had gone. The wreck looked very lacking in their absence. Conducting a tour of the wreck I studied a single cream plumerose anemone on which the plume tilted in the current. Then things really picked up when under a huge winch I encountered a lovely John Dory with its incredible dorsal fin standing proud. Next a feeding colony of bright and tightly packed red jewel anemones on the winch kept my shutter finger alive.

A proud John Dory *Zeus faber* extends its magnificent dorsal fin in defensive action (The *Royal Adelaide*)

An amusing close tompot blenney portrait (The *Royal Adelaide*)

A small dahlia anemone *Urticina felina* amid large pebbles (Chesil Beach)

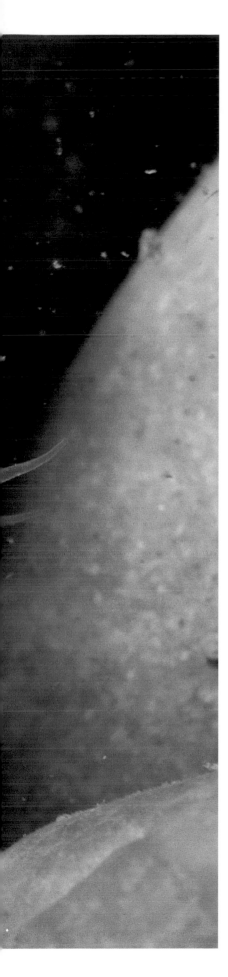

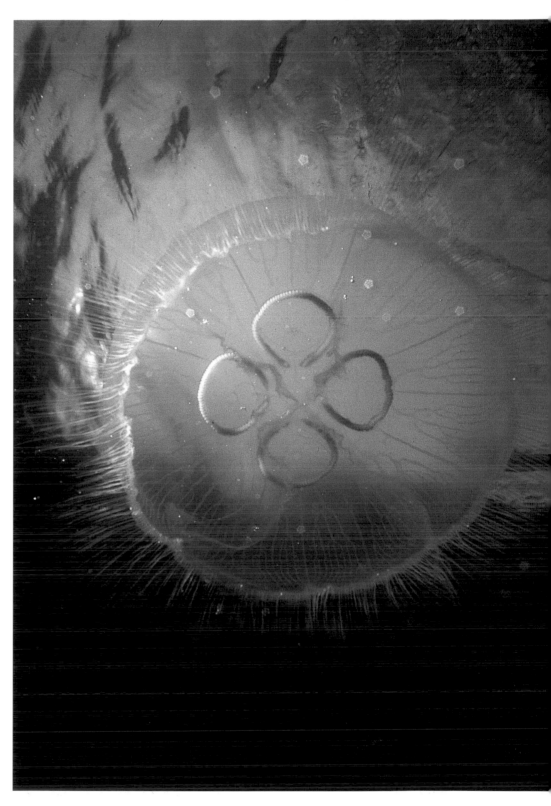

A moon jellyfish *Aurelia aurita* reaches the top of its cycle at the surface (Chesil Beach)

I finished my film, taking macro images of the feeding mantle of mussels and the little white barnacles that live on them. These abundant mollusc I had seen on many dives, but had previously never given them time as a subject. I was disappointed when I first reached the *Royal Adelaide* that day, but the wreck proved to have many other features worthy of my attention with some very interesting images achieved.

CHAPTER 8
Lundy Island

*A*s I slipped under the water of a calm blue sea, two seals were playing on the surface. They splashed about sending out ripples across the small shallow bay. I swam in their direction checking my camera equipment as I went. Finding them was easy in the clear water as they played around at the surface. As I slowly approached, one saw me and swam gracefully down to meet me. It moved all around, eyes checking things out. A few moments later sensing no threat, it moved in gradually until its widespread soft nose was flat against my mask and its whiskers were brushing my face. As I put out my hand it rolled over in a submissive stance. It grunted with pleasure as I tickled its large, smooth tummy. I played with this seal for fifteen minutes without taking a single image and was totally bowled over by the experience of this – my first unforgettable grey seal encounter.

A grey seal pup gracefully turns in front of the camera in the Devil's Kitchen

I exited the water from 'The Devil's Kitchen', following an experience that would be hard to beat and with a roll of seal shots in the can. The afternoon sunlight had shone down through the calm, clear water producing dancing surface reflections on both the seals and the cordweed surroundings. I had gained supreme satisfaction from this encounter, which was without doubt enhanced by the fact that the seals had reacted just as positively to the experience. A wonderful rendezvous indeed!

All this had occurred within an hour of arriving on Lundy Island. Both visiting the island and diving with grey seals had been high on my hit list for the last two years. Travelling from Bideford with freelance film-maker Andy Hibbert, we disembarked from the HMS *Oldenburg* on a beautiful day to be met by the welcoming faces of Phil Robertson and Marcus Heyes. Introductions and hand-shakes were barely completed before Marcus had excitedly informed us about the two seals that were playing with snorkellers in 'The Devil's Kitchen' and did we want to dive right away! Doing just that had produced a spectacular intro-duction to Lundy Island.

Diving this lovely bay again later in the week, I spent quite some time getting close to a magnificent young John Dory. This vibrant fish's gilded yellow hues, undulated markings and prominent central 'eye' were the most vivid that I had ever seen. Watching it hunting small two-spot gobies, it always faced its prey head on. This presented the fish as only a slender pencil-like shape that was lost amongst the cordweed. It conducted a sort of erratic victory dance on the one occasion I saw a successful hunt. Patience was rewarded for both of us perhaps, for it was finally just inches in front of my wide-angle lens. Heading inshore

A grey seal turns at the surface after taking a breath of fresh air in the Devil's Kitchen

towards the end of this dive, I took in the vista of this lovely bay. The late afternoon sun created a dramatic surface detail backdrop to the flowing vertical growth of cordweed, with lime-green sea lettuce growing tighter to the rocks. Was this the same Bristol Channel that flows murky and lifeless close to my home?

The Devil's Kitchen and the landing bay provide the only available shore dives. Steep cliffs rising to a plateaux, which averages over a hundred metres high, dominate the rest of the island making boat diving the order of the day.

As our days on Lundy passed we were blessed with superb summer weather. Andy and I had joined Philip and Marcus for the last week of their month-long marine archaeological study of Lundy and some of its recorded 216 shipwrecks. Our task was to produce a photographic record to illustrate their work. The archaeological work took priority during our dives, but the enthusiasm for marine life of all parties kept us in the water long past the time required for the project. Some days we spent more than twelve hours in Philip's RIB, eventually crawling back up the long, steep track in the dark to the island's *Marisco* tavern, having first made desperate mobile phone pleas for much-needed late food.

A fine young John Dory watched while hunting two-spot gobies in the Devil's Kitchen

Lundy is one of the few locations in Britain where all five British corals can be found. I photographed my first treasured pictures of the rare British sunset coral here on the north-facing vertical wall of the canyon formed by the famous Knoll Pins. This spectacular and photogenic bright yellow-orange cup coral evaded me on my first efforts to seek it out. I contented myself photographing a white and pink Devonshire cup coral that was nicely separated from the reef by its contrasting colours. A fully extended and feeding subtle pink jewel anemone was next to fill my frame, its position allowed me to bracket the direction of strobe lighting between images for later assessment. Then a false alarm when a colony of particularly bright orange *Parazoanthus* came into view. They were, none the less, a lovely subject that used the rest of my film experimenting with their compositional merits. A little later in the day, re-entering the water with the intent on finding my illusive subject, I swam between the two pinnacles and descended

Close details of a tight colony of *Parazoanthus* anemones (The Knoll Pins)

straight down into a dark, moody canyon. The search was quickly over for this fortunately proved to be the location of the sunset corals. I set to work recording images of this aptly named little gem, with planned full-frame macro images showing good composition and important details. My strobe spotting light picked out all the coral's merits – it really was a stunning subject; I admired the way the colours embraced. The bright orange of the prominent central mouth forked outwards fading between the ever-searching bright yellow tapering tentacles. These semi-transparent tentacles showed the denser yellow details of hundreds of tiny loaded stinging cells ready to capture prey. While the ever-hungry billowing central mouth was always waiting to be fed.

Right:
Close detail of a single feeding jewel anemone *Corynactis viridis* (The Knoll Pins)

Close details of the rare British sunset coral *Leptopsammia* (The Knoll Pins)

A little farther north along the east coast of Lundy is the equally famous and productive dive site of Gannet's Rock. My eyes and ears took in this location prior to an early morning dive in a calm, unmoving sea. The island of Lundy lay before me like an emerald projecting from the deep-blue Atlantic Ocean. The rising sun brought out the colours and hues of the island's flora and dramatically-shaped granite rocks. Puffins, guillemots and gannets created the only sounds, save for the odd exchange of grunts from seals hauling out of the water to appreciate the warmth of the morning sun. The ambience of this island was amazing. I rolled back into the sea, appreciating the environment that had produced such an admirable start to my day.

I passed pure white feeding dead mens' fingers that were nicely contrasted by endless colonies of jewel anemones. While photographing an unusual composition of plumerose anemones, I was suddenly aware of a little movement from a widespread pair of brown eyes. They belonged to a multi-coloured, thick-lipped scorpion fish that was self-assured its camouflage retained its presence unseen. Capturing a few close portraits I left it hidden on the reef still waiting for smaller prey.

From colours that camouflage position to colours that emphasise it, jewel anemones come in such a range of colours that some of them look quite surreal.

A beautiful *Antiopella cristata* nudibranch battles its way across an undulating kelp frond (Gannet's Rock)

A child might colour a creature bright yellow, lime green, translucent gold and purple, perhaps describing a dream, but when nature paints a picture in this way, it creates an incredible scene. Consider a bright antiopella nudibranch fighting its way across an olive kelp frond that was constantly moving in an increasing current. Fighting with all of these elements, I used the rest of my film and all of my frustrated patience to capture an image justifying the incredible detail that this subject displayed. Above and below the water, Lundy was displaying its natural charm.

The wreck of a coaster, the *Robert*, lies in 25 metres of water 2 kilometres out from The Knoll Pins and this photogenic wreck is popular with most visiting divers. It is virtually intact and lies on its starboard side on a flat, sandy bottom. Distinctive features, such as companionway ladders, winches, cargo hold vents and handrails, are all adorned with anemones. I came across a conger eel whose home was a squeeze inside a small vent tube. It did not seem perturbed by my close attentions, indeed, after several minutes it literally 'yawned' the suggestion, 'Isn't it time you moved on to other things?'

Below right:
A companionway ladder is colonised by anemones feeding from the passing current on the wreck of the *Robert*.

Below:
A pink and white feeding Devonshire cup coral *Caryophyllia smithii* stands proudly against the reef (The Knoll Pins)

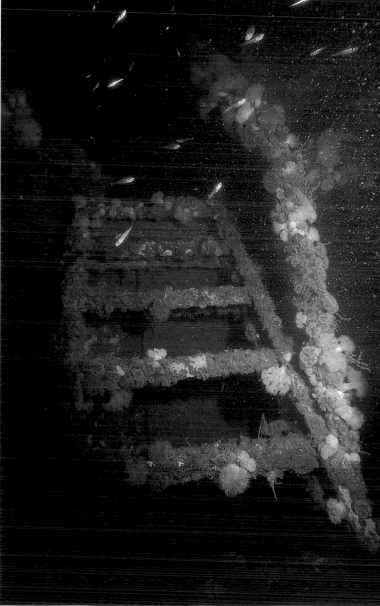

Another star of the *Robert* is a really crusty old lobster that excavated its home under the stern section at least eight years ago. If approached, this heavy clawed character immediately stages its forward and reverse impressions of a powerful bulldozer. The mass of broken shells all around serve notice to avoid its massive claws. Patrolling cuckoo wrasse, ballen wrasse, and large shoals of pollack and bib complete the impressive marine life that the *Robert* displays so well.

Opposite:
A group of mixed coloured feeding plumerose anemones *Metridium senile* (Gannet's Rock)

This wily old lobster *Homarus gammarus* has been living and excavating under the keel of the *Robert* for at least eight years

A young lobster *Homarus gammarus* on the wreck of the *Amstralstroom*

The rugged and inaccessible west coast of the island shows the ravages of south-westerly storms. In fine conditions it was difficult for me to imagine what sea conditions could be like here. Shipwrecks were quickly pounded to pieces by huge 'pebbles', some exceeding one metre round. Massive seas then scattered the unidentifiable remains amongst deep-scoured granite gullies. In contrast to this, we spent endless hours diving the area at a very leisurely pace. During our last day we had already spent over five hours enjoying the diving within a small bay between Battery Point and Dead Cow Point. Marcus and I were soaking up the sun's rays in the boat while following the bubbles of Phil and Andy. We both quickly reacted as three heads returned to the surface. It turned out that a superb young seal would not leave them alone and had completely disrupted their survey. It's a hard life being a marine archaeologist!

All pleased with our day's 'work', we were finally making headway to return to the landing bay when Marcus shouted 'There she blows!', suggesting that it was not yet all over. He had spotted the tail and dorsal fin of a large basking shark circling on the surface. As we approached, Andy, Marcus and I slipped into the water. Trying to keep up with or predicting the path of the shark was not easy. For, just like the grey seals, the basking shark, complete with three large remoras, showed superiority in its environment and quite easily gave me the slip. But Andy refused to be beaten. He was a zealous cameraman with the scent of some good footage and I am sure he would have followed the shark around the island had it not finally disappeared into the depths. He eventually exited the water totally dead beat, but he had finished his trip the same as mine had started, with a marine life ambition fulfilled.

A camouflaged sea scorpion *Taurulus bubalis* waits patiently for passing prey (Gannet's Rock)

CHAPTER 9
St Abbs Marine Reserve

L ooking up towards the surface, I watched the early morning sun rise over a kelp-covered boulder. The still air above the surface produced a smooth rippling sea. This, together with the low angle of the sun, created a fine example of 'snail's window'. The lighter arc-shaped area of penetrating light mirrored the circle of kelp below, but contrasted its silhouetted image. The darker surface area of reflected light placed a pleasing balanced diagonal of separation across this phenomenon. I captured my love of the early morning sea.

Before continuing on out into Leeds Bay I admired the resilience of red and green beadlet anemones. They spent most of their time feeding in the cold sea, coping with surf and swell. They also had to endure many hours in high temperatures above the low water line, perhaps even being in the direct rays of the sun. They protected their mouth and tentacles by covering them with a mucus-covered foot.

An early morning sunlight forms a 'snail's window' effect over a calm sea that mirrors the silhouetted shape of a kelp-covered reef (Leeds Bay)

A beautifully patterned, snake-like butterfish slipped timidly through the underwater jungle, its form broken up by colour contrast. Time and not just a little patience were spent trying to predict its path. Eventually, with care and consideration, its tiny head accepted being within the inch gap of my 2-1 macro probes.

Moving on out around the headland I turned in the direction of Weasel Loch. Crossing a sandy bay towards a dark cave, I came across a camouflaged flatfish lying on a sandy sea-bed that contained flecks of red and white shell and the occasional high relief of lugworms' dark sand casts. Nature had repainted the sea-bed on the back of this stationary fish.

Defending the large cave entrance was a little northern prawn that used its feelers to bravely 'fence' off my offending macro probes as I carefully attempted to gain a picture. Though lacking the 'rugby socks' feature of common prawns, the red flash 'war paint' of this northern variety is very photogenic and worthy of a little attention. Eventually, after capturing a few frames, I decided to make my retreat. The brave prawn stood proud in victory, having won yet another war!

Swimming on towards Weasel Loch, I saw two divers heading in my direction. Their movement was erratic, one of continuous stops and goes. It turned out that they were being very inconsiderate by constantly harassing a slow-swimming,

Close details of a northern prawn *Pandalus montagui* (Leeds Bay)

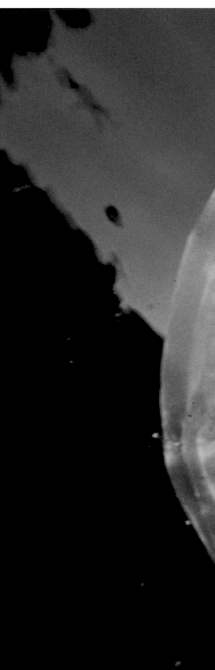

bottom-dwelling angler fish that made various abortive attempts to evade them. I took just a single image as it passed not wanting to add to its dilemma. I likened its surreal appearances to that of the 'Star Ship *Enterprise*'. I signalled to the divers that they should slow down, but they simply pointed to the fish and carried on with their chase. My angry thoughts were 'Beam them up, Scotty' and get them educated out of this marine reserve!

Hugging the bottom as I turned into Weasel Loch to complete the last stage of my dive, the ambient light was getting lower and lower. Bemused, I looked up towards the surface 10 metres above, but I could not see it because the possible combination of a rising wind and current had funnelled thousands of moon jelly-fish into the small loch. At my exit point, this phenomenon had gathered them three feet thick at the surface. It was an incredible sight at the completion of my dive, but I had to get out of the water. Purging my Octopus regulator from the depleting contents of my cylinder I eventually cleared a hole allowing my 'escape'.

Three members of the Bristol Underwater Photography Group, Andrew Sawyer Parker, Alan Mildren and myself, approached the small, picturesque fishing village of St Abbs. Save for the seagulls and us, all were still sleeping. We had arrived early to maximise our plans for the day. Andrew and I were assisting Alan Mildren as model divers in his current AV production of the St Abbs' marine reserve.

The sun shines through the surface water and an egg-bearing translucent moon jellyfish *Aurelia aurita* (Weasel Loch)

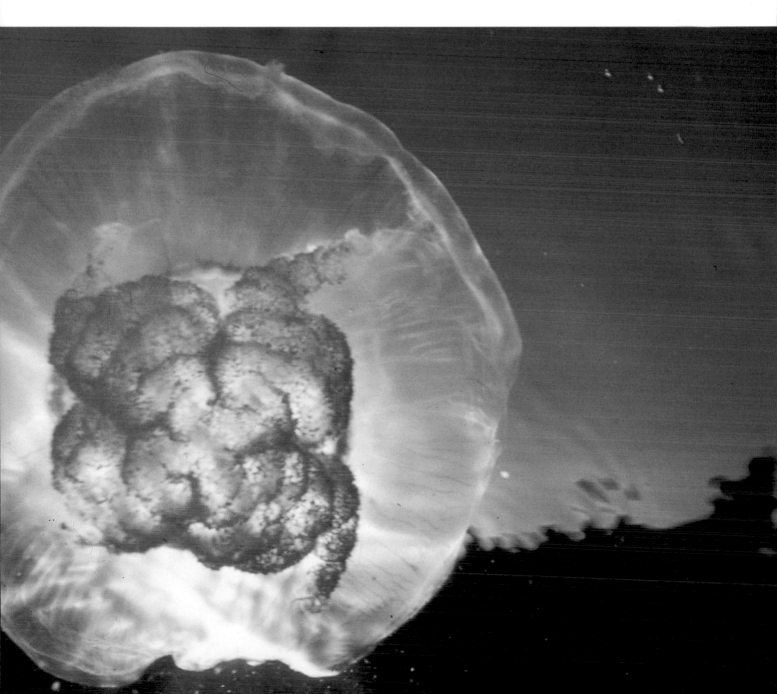

The head of lovely butterfish *Pholisgunnellus* is finally just inches in front of the lens (Leeds Bay)

Nature has painted the sea-bed on the back of this wonderful plaice *Pleuronectes platessa* (Leeds Bay)

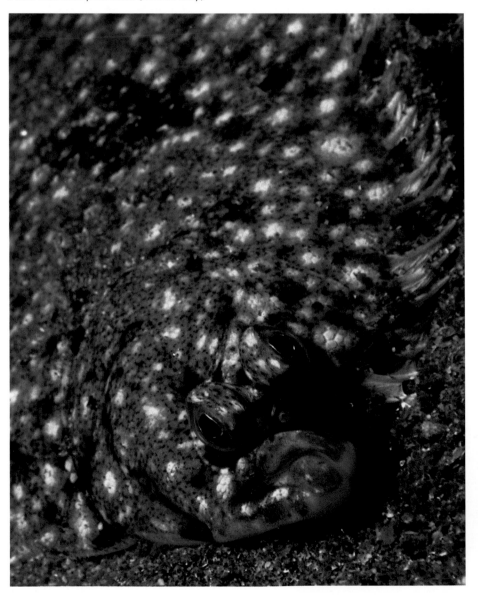

A feeding beadlet anemone *Actinia equina* stretches with its tentacles catching food in the shallows of Leeds Bay

Justifiably reputed as one of the most spectacular shore dives in the UK, 'Cathedral Arch' lies just outside the harbour. We were all familiar with diving this area. Our plans were to proceed directly to Cathedral Arch to carry out various sequences and return to the harbour via a beautiful kelp gully to complete an 'exit scene'. At final completion of this work, which took a little longer than expected (it always does!), we returned to Cathedral Arch for Andrew and I to complete images considered during an earlier visit.

The sheer size of Cathedral Arch is not easy to portray on film. You are always at the mercy of light levels and horizontal visability to achieve distant shots that have inherent lighting and colour loss problems. I opted to capture each side of the arch in turn. One side allowed the opportunity to include the naturally-lit distant top arch with one of many resident mature male ballen wrasse swimming through it. On the other side I captured Alan Mildren recording static marine life near the top of the lower arch.

The roof of the top arch contains an unusual feature, perhaps normally related to wrecks. In this case the exhaled air of visiting divers becomes trapped by a large pocket within the non-porous rock. I was keen to achieve rippled reflection images of a diver's intrigue of this feature. Cathedral Arch is also famous for its fine examples of mature male ballen wrasse that are very diver-friendly. I wanted images of these normally territorial males unnatural tolerance of each other. Heading back to the harbour via the sunlit kelp gullies, I stopped to admire the extraordinary long and abundant tentacles of a common Scottish urchin. As I worked, the sea suddenly went dramatically darker and looking up I saw a large *Cyanea lamarckii* jellyfish, which appeared uncannily similar to a small bulbous grey cloud that had temporarily covered the sun.

On our last morning the wind came up from the south-east. This precluded diving from Eyemouth and St Abbs, but the reserve has the benefit of north-facing Petticowick, an incredibly wild and beautiful part of this coastline that can cope with a limited number of divers. Within this fairly shallow bay the shingle sea-bed is liberally covered by larger rocks and boulders harbouring all forms of bottom-dwelling life.

Watching a polycera nudibranch rasping away on a colony of sea mat, I

Below left:
A swimming angler fish *Lophius piscatorius* creates a serious Starship *Enterprise* guise (Leeds Bay)

admired its vivid colours contrasting against the background of a swaying olive kelp frond. These advertised colours obviously stated 'Don't eat me if you want to stay healthy'. My subject was approached head on by another nudibranch. After touching tentacles, and perhaps chemically establishing they were the same species, they locked into a typical polycera head-to-tail, side-mounted embrace to ensure the survival of their species. Large common sunstar displayed their colours from large rocks and an orange and cream *Solaster endeca* starfish endlessly hunted in this interesting terrain. Pairs of mating hermit crabs covered in cloak anemone looked comical as they scurried around holding 'hands'.

Below:
Diving photographer Andrew Sawyer Parker enters the top of Cathedral Arch (St Abbs)

A common sunstar *Crossaster upapposus* creates a blaze of colour on a large rock (Petticowick)

A fine pair of tolerant male ballen wrasse *labrus bergylta* at the base of Cathedral Arch (St Abbs)

An orange-cream coloured *Solaster endeca* starfish hunts over a vertical reef (Petticowick)

Glowing, long tentacles on a common sea urchin *Echinus esclentus* (St Abbs)

Most dive destinations can usually produce a surprise or two. On turning back towards my exit point I had good fortune with my first sighting of a superb pinkish-orange hued *Bolocera tuediac*. On one hand I was delighted, for this subject is normally found in far deeper waters. On the other I was frustrated, having just a single precious frame left to secure an image from this chance encounter. I cursed, not for the first time in my life, the fact that this was to be the last dive prior to our return to Bristol.

Heading inshore, I surfaced near an old jetty and removed my fins to exit. On the opposite side of the beach where sheer rock cliffs rise from the sea, the frantic calls of two trapped lambs attracted their mother's attention. Maternal instinct insisted that she get to them, but, alas, she crashed 50 feet into a shallow sea. Knocked out by the fall, the sheep suddenly came round and thrashed blindly about at the surface. Putting my fins back on I had one more thing to do – complete my first, and hopefully last, 'surface' rescue.

A common sunstar *Crossaster upapposus* creates a blaze of colour on a large rock (Petticowick)

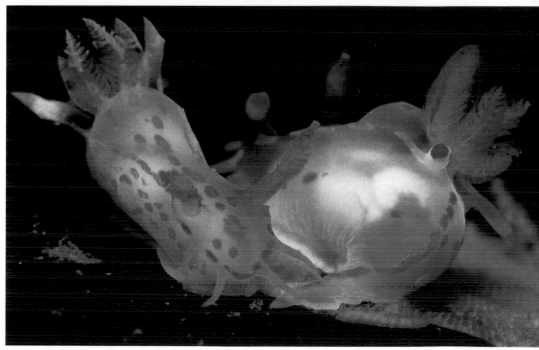

A pair of *Polycera sp* nudibranch mating on a contrasting kelp frond (Petticowick)

CHAPTER 10
The Sound of Mull

Looking back across the Sound of Mull towards Lochaline, a southerly gale was howling directly towards it. The high cliffs form the area to the right of Lochaline dominating the coastline from Ardtornish Point to Rubha an Ridire. Five or six waterfalls cascade over these cliffs, draining water from Glais Bheinn way above. In the lee afforded by the close mountains of the Isle of Mull, Alan Mildren and I prepared to dive. My eyes kept returning to the cliffs across the Sound to watch fast flowing waterfalls turn upwards, snaking into the sky, due to the strength of the wind in that exposed area. Entering the water, I descending to the bottom, but all I could visualise was incredible waterfalls going up.

I progressed slowly through a low density kelp forest, still thinking about the vista above. It took the brilliant red of a fine cushionstar to kick my photography into gear. This short-armed and beefy-looking starfish beckoned my attention as

A red cushionstar *Porania pulvillus* explores close to a small colony of featherstars (Ardtornish Point)

I dropped down over a reef. Moving in closer I realised that in front of the cushionstar was an incredibly well-camouflaged sea scorpion. It mimicked the surrounding reef to perfection, making it difficult to portray. A top lighting angle produced contrast by placing a dark shadow under its head.

Moving on, another cushionstar created better contrast on a black rocky sea-bed and was nicely colour co-ordinated by a group of small featherstars. Larger individual featherstars sought out vantage points alone. I worked a bright yellow specimen with all its arms searching upwards and its numerous cirri precariously held on to the flat surface of a projecting rock in the current. Another formed a very pleasing composition, gracefully gripping a vertical kelp stem. I was impressed yet again when its widespread arms resembled an exploding sky rocket each time they were lit by my strobe.

As I slowly ascended to the surface, I blended my surreal sightings – a water-fall snaked up into a night sky lit by a dazzling exploding featherstar. Back in the real world at the surface, the wind was picking up the waves and throwing them at Alan and Philip in the boat. It was passed the time to be at sea and we quickly headed for the shore, all enjoying the fun as Phil's RIB surfed the fast-moving waves through the narrow channel into Loch Aline.

Below right:
Brittlestars *Ophiothrix fragilis* escape over the top of a large hunting common sunstar *Crossaster papposus* (Lochaline wall)

Below:
An incredibly well-camouflaged sea scorpion *Taurulus bubalis* waits for passing prey on Ardtornish Point reef

A yellow featherstar *Antedon bifida* clings to a smooth rock in strong current
using its numerous cirri (Ardtornish Point reef)

The unique wreck of the *Thesis* lies in shallow water close to the shore at the east end of Inninmore Bay. It reminded me of an intact fish skeleton where the bones had been picked clean to expose rows of projecting arched ribs. Many years ago, this wreck had been 'picked clean' of its valuable steel plates by salvers. The remaining rows of ribs are adorned with thousands of multi-coloured filter feeders. All were taking advantage of the high relief of this wreck, which now allows the prevailing current to pass right through it. Large shoals of small pollack slowly meandered through the ribs, heading into the current to pick off passing prey. Phil Robertson kindly afforded me some diver interaction as he surveyed this skeletal scene.

Just outside the small, deep channel that links Loch Aline to the Sound is an impressive vertical wall. A sounding the previous day had shown 94 metres of water just 25 feet out from shore. A big drop off by any standards. Alan Mildren's spotting light rapidly faded and disappeared as he descended down into the gloom. Stepping off the edge of this 300-foot vertical cliff, I flew down the wall to join him.

The wall had lots of ledges and holes that afforded protection to dozens of long-clawed squat lobsters. In shallow water these lobsters are normally nocturnal, but the light levels in this depth were close to the dark of night. The lobsters were very active and quite prepared to do battle, with extended open claws whenever approached on their territorial ground. Time at depth went by too quickly as I considered how to light their aggressive display.

A long-clawed squat lobster protects its territory way down the Lochaline wall

Moving back up the reef I watched a hunting sunstar claw its way up a vertical overhang. Another had found several fast-moving brittlestars that cleverly avoided its ever-hungry mouth by escaping across its back. But eventually the sunstar catches its prey, retracting its fourteen legs to retain it. Spending a little time at 5 metres, I was still in the company of a sunstar. This time its vivid colours co-ordinated with the coralline colours of the natural light at the top of the wall. Looking down into the blackness, I recalled the subjects, colours and natural events I had seen on this amazing wall.

Diving, like many other equipment-intensive and technical sports, has moments of frustration when such equipment fails you. On a fine morning with all our equipment stowed, we headed north-west along the Sound of Mull towards Tobermory. We were all fired up and looking forward to our first dive on the famous wreck of the *Hispania*, reputed by many to be the best preserved wreck in Scottish waters. Imagine our frustration and horror when, within sight of the *Hispania* marker buoy, the outboard engine made an awful noise, put a conrod through the engine casing and died!

When Philip had finished explaining to the engine what he thought of it, we gave it a few minutes silence while looking around the now empty Sound for a non-existent tow. There was only one thing for it – we rowed an unimpressive course north across the Sound to Rhemore. Philip and Alan thumbed a lift the six miles back into Lochaline to prepare and return with a small standby inflatable. I consoled myself snapping away a few frames on sea pens in shallow water.

Fifty years of corrosion has taken its toll on the *Hispania*'s handrails

120

As time went by I quite enjoyed the solitude, reflecting on the quality of diving in the Sound. The day turned towards dusk and I was considering a night dive when I heard the sound of Phil's little stand-by boat. For the next hour we completed a moonlit salvage tow back through the Sound to Lochaline.

The next morning was our last in the Sound, so, following hurried engine and linkage change, our intrepid band were back on the sea once again making headway for the *Hispania*. With a sense of final arrival we tied onto the buoy and descended onto the wreck. Sitting upright and fairly intact on the sea-bed in 25 to 30 metres it makes a very impressive dive. I travelled along the entire starboard side of this multi-coloured anemone-encrusted wreck. But by doing so in the time available it was impossible to photograph all of its nautical features.

At the bows I framed the arc of steel where the hull forms the forecastle, showing adjoining handrails and bollards. Moving on down the foredeck, corroded handrails had been eaten by nearly fifty years of rust. In front of the second cargo hatch impressive winches and twin masts set a moody scene. Beside a long-gone porthole from the midships superstructure, neatly coiled rigging is covered in life and a buckled ladder rises to a non-existent deckhead. Finally the intact and eerie stern superstructure is viewed from outside of its handrails. Slipping reluctantly back up the buoy line, I watched the wreck disappear in the gloom. I promised myself I would return one day to the *Hispania* to capture more of its prominent features.

Marine life now takes the place of salvaged steel plates on the ribs of the wreck of the *Thesis*

As our diving was completed, we took advantage of the good weather with a leisurely route back to Lochaline hugging the north coast. We cut our engines and drifted into a small bay near Fiunary and watched several inquisitive seal pups playing in clear, calm waters. A little further on where a large stream entered the sea, we silently paddled the RIB to within 20 feet of an otter feasting on velvet swimming crab near the water. Finally hearing us above the noise of crunching crab, it stood on its hind legs to take a good look at us before disappearing under a flurry of expanding ripples. Once again the wild terrain in the Sound of Mull had provided unforgettable displays of nature.

A moody image of a long-gone porthole and stowed rigging (The *Hispania*)

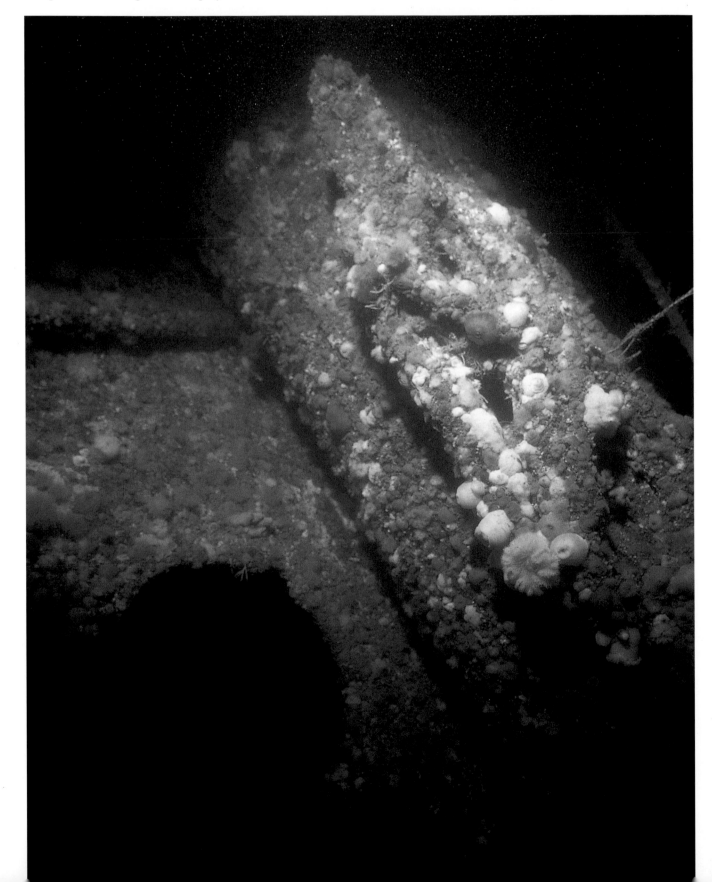

CHAPTER 11
The Summer Isles

W ay up in the north-west of Scotland the thirty or so unpopulated Summer Isles (Tanera Mór being the exception) lie scattered through 5 square miles of often turbulent sea, just off the windy, exposed coast from Achiltibuie. The islands can always provide a lee shore to the prevailing south-west and westerly winds for safe diving, providing adequate boat facilities are available to reach them. Water quality can be excellent even in bad weather, with underwater visibility around 20 metres. Maximum spring tides of 4 metres rarely created tidal streams of more than half a knot. This excellent location provides impressive underwater cliffs, large boulder slopes, pinnacles and mearl beds all with their own generous share of marine life.

Marine archaeologist Philip Robertson, AV photographer Alan Mildren and I have worked together on several projects over the last few years, becoming both dive buddies and firm friends. During a July 1995 project on Lundy Island, Philip related to me his desire to dive 'Conservation Cave' located on the south side of his family-owned island of Tanera Beg. He had spent much of his youth and school holidays happily exploring Tanera Beg down to the shore line and now had an understandably strong hankering to explore it from under the sea. We finally completed this appealing exercise at the end of October, much later in the year than we intended. We were then introduced to some challenging Summer Isles diving.

Close details of featherstars *Antedon bifida* and seasquirts *Ciona intestinalis* colonising a kelp stipe (Tanera Mór boulder slope)

A stormy plumerose anemone and kelp-covered pinnacle scene (Sqeir A Chapuill)

The top of Eilean A Char decorated with dead mens' fingers *Alcyonium digitatum* and climbing common sea urchins *Echinus esculentus*

We moored Philip's boat in a small picturesque harbour sheltered by the close Isle of Ristol and enjoyed both the hospitality and laid back character of the local fishermen that carefully extracted a living from these dangerous and windy seas. During our five days of diving, we left the safety of this small haven intent on diving Tanera Beg's 'Conservation Cave', but for three and a half days the sea beat us back and forced us into the lee of the northern shores.

At a site called Sqeir A Chapuill, huge colonies of plumerose anemones occupied every available space on the tops of two pinnacles and these, together with wild, irregular kelp movement and strong surface wave details, created a dramatic, untamed spectacle. Dropping down one of these pinnacles I admired the pleasing images of a proud dahlia anemone at the base of a small vertical rock face covered in featherstars. Suddenly, having that uncanny feeling of being watched, I looking up expecting to see the grinning face of my dive buddy Alan Mildren waiting to give me a fright. What I saw was far more pretty and pleasing, for sat on the top of the rock was a blushing pink curled octopus that looked almost embarrassed for peeping. This friendly subject sat with its tentacles turned underneath itself. It flushed through pastel colours as I moved slowly in gaining its trust. It finally allowing me to concentrate macro images around its incredible rectangular eyes. As I left, it slipped down over the rock to inspect the dahlia anemone that first attracted my attention. What an intelligent marine life encounter!

On the north-west side of Tanera Mór we dived on a 20-metre boulder slope with mearl covering the sea-bed. At the top of the slope in the kelp zone, kelp stipes appeared over 6 inches thick due to a prolific influx of featherstars and sea

A dahlia anemone *Urticina felina* below featherstars *Antedon bifida* at the bottom of Sqeir A Chapuill pinnacle

squirts that capitalised their high relief. Yet more featherstars swam to join them, using undulating arms to gain the required height in the passing tide.

I stopped and watched some incredible action as a large, bright orange, seven-armed starfish charged through a living sea-bed of common brittlestar that writhed over each other to escape. The overall effect of this movement looked just like an expanding ship's wake.

A kelp-topped wall at Eilean A Char was decorated with dead mens' fingers and climbing urchins. This wall was a series of large ledges down to 30 metres, creating habitats for lobsters and prawns. A fine orange and russet spiny starfish demanded my attention, its curled arms highly contrasted by the ledge behind it covered in coralline algae. My final frames of this dive were directed at the prolific abundance of bottom-dwelling life. A small group of white seasquirts looked as if they were being choked out of existence by a dual attack from both featherstars and brittlestars.

During our fourth day, following a memorable dive with nine grey seals on the north side of Eilean A Char, the sky cleared of clouds and the wind faded away to create a window in the weather allowing us to finally fulfil Philip's quest. The afternoon saw us heading for 'Conservation Cave'. Our cameras, tanks and

A featherstar swims to gain the height of kelp stipes (Tanera Mór boulder slope)

tummies had all been filled for the task ahead. As we rounded the headland, turning east along the wild south coast, the cave presented a very dominant feature. Huge columns of rock supported its sloping roof that towered above the sea. Large Atlantic swells entered the cave to thunder against unyielding vertical rear walls that repelled them back out into a confused sea.

As Philip prepared to lead the first dive his face was full of the pleasure of a man about to fulfil a long-term ambition. He disappeared beneath the waves expectantly clutching his camera. He eventually returned to the surface to exclaim, 'Wonderful, absolutely wonderful.'

Opposite:
A seven-armed starfish *Luidia ciliaris* causes panic among a huge colony of common brittle-stars *Ophiothrix fragilis* (Tanera Mór boulder slope)

A common starfish *Asterias rubens* climbs a rock occupied by a closed dead mens' finger *Alcyonium digitatum* (Sqeir A Chapuill)

An orange-russet coloured spiny starfish *Marthasterias glacialis* explores a rock crevice deco-rated with coralline algae (Eilean A Char)

Keen to experience this cave for myself, I soon slipped under the waves. The smooth shapes of the cave floor had been sculptured by endless years of Atlantic swells and were now carpeted by a brilliant patchwork of coralline algae. Large static rocks had fallen from the ageing roof to feature in a central location. Open spaces were filled with urchins, velvet swimming crabs and common starfish that quickly consumed a generous supply of broken mussels dislodged from the cave walls by the pounding swell. Shock waves from this pounding sent out constant reminders not to foul up on our buoyancy control.

Long, natural cracks in the rock faces of both floors and walls were filled to overflowing with multi-coloured dahlia anemones. They mimicked an aerial view of the crowded motorway madness so often seen on the summer season TV news. Velvet swimming crabs, prawns and sea spiders attended this scene, clearing away any accident debris.

The morning of our last day was also spent at 'Conservation Cave', but a worsening swell decreed diver movement of up to 10 feet either side of any potential static subject making good photography almost impossible and survival a bit of a challenge. Deciding that discretion was more appropriate than valour, I exited the cave to explore the surrounding terrain.

Close up of seven-armed starfish *Luidia ciliaris* (Tanera Mór boulder slope)

The blushing colours of a curled octopus *Eledone cirrhosa* contrast the reef at the bottom of Sqeir A Chapuill

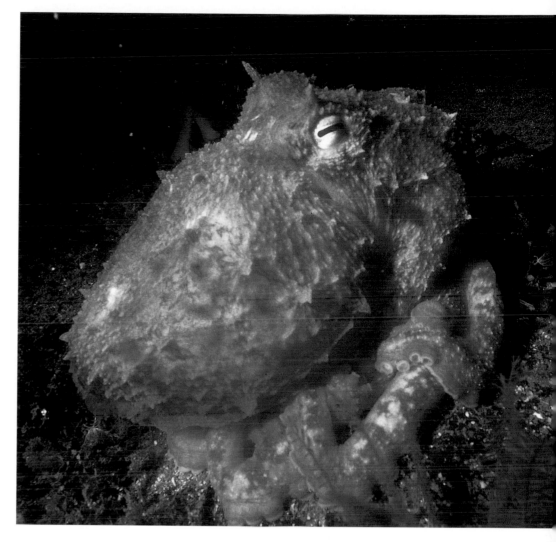

Close details of the curled octopus's incredible rectangular speckled eye (Sqeir A Chapuill)

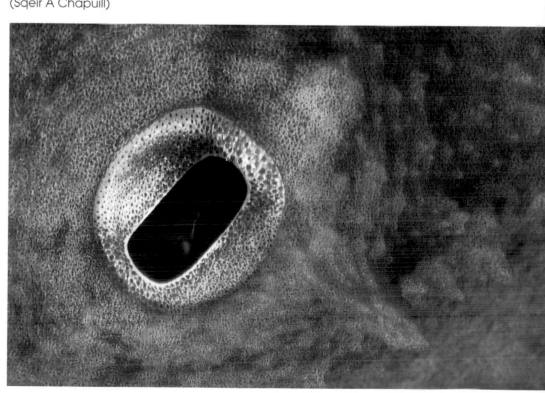

Opposite:
Seasquirts *Ciona intestinalis* seemed choked by a bed of featherstars *Antedon bifida* and brittlestars *Ophiothrix fragilis* (Eilean A Char)

Below:
Dahlia anemones *Urticina felina* and common starfish *Asterias rubens* adorn coralline algae-covered rocks in Conservation Cave (Tanera Beg)

I ended up travelling through an area of huge intimidating storm-worn boulders. This fact, together with the now huge Atlantic swells, not only made for exciting diving but also created the awesome feeling of being part of a film set for the movie *Honey, I Shrunk the Kids.* On my arrival back at the surface I was quite relieved to see that at least Philip's smiling face and the dive boat were relevant to my size!

All good diving expeditions have to finally come to an end. Later that day as we stowed away our equipment back at Philip's family croft on the mainland at Achiltibuie, Alan and I discussed the daunting prospects of our long night journey back to Bristol. Philip walked into the lounge and opened the croft's traditional visitors book and asked us to 'Write a wee verse'. Taking time to reflect on this recent adventure I wrote:

> We came from afar, to the windy wild west,
> To capture some images of sea life at best,
> We fought with the weather, the surf, and the swell,
> To explore the Summer Isles, at times it was hell
> Our efforts were rewarded, as our adventures unfold,
> Cavernous caves, seals and sunstars, ours to behold,
> We went home with the images that were our quest,
> And fond memories of diving the windy wild west.

Opposite:
A dahlia anemone *Urticina felina* finds solitude high on a coralline algae-covered vertical wall of Conservation Cave (Tanera Beg)

A velvet swimming crab *Uliocarinus puber* scavenges damaged mussels trapped on the sides of dahlia anemones *Urticina felina* (Conservation Cave, Tanera Beg)

CHAPTER 12
Underwater Photography

Many fine books have been written regarding this challenging subject. Most of them I have read at one time or another and from each have extracted various priceless pearls of wisdom that have worked for me and broadened my photographic potential. I believe that most underwater photographers develop their skills through such books and gleaning information from others and perhaps emulating their work. An open mind is then required to decide what information suites your developing personal approach at any given time.

Text books and theory afford the technical ability to operate sometimes complex equipment, but at the end of the day there is no substitute for spending the maximum possible time within the marine environment and sharpening your practical skills by working with both the equipment and the challenging wildlife subjects. The art in your photography grows from these skills, to be polished by your personal taste, dedication and a critical analysis of results while striving for a particular effect or image.

The turbid waters of the British coast can be potentially very dangerous. It is therefore imperative that full diving skills are achieved and that a budding underwater photographer is at one with this alien environment long before accepting the attention demanded by underwater photography.

Any technical, manual or auto constraints imposed on your photography will vary according the equipment you can afford to buy or have made available to yourself. Do not feel that you cannot succeed without the latest and most expensive all-singing and all-dancing state-of-the-art equipment – because you can! My philosophy is one of learning to get the best from the equipment available to you, 'brownie points' awarded through improvising manufacturers' equipment with personal modifications that cost only a little time to create a whole new range of effects. I have been using Nikonos 111s, 1VAs and Vs with various cheap strobe units for ten years and have yet to exhaust personal ideas on accessories to enhance their use.

My personal approach to underwater photography has developed into one of manual control for 90 per cent of exposures taken. In my early years I relied totally on auto-camera functions and TTL strobe control without really getting to understand what exposure, F.s and strobe guide numbers were all about. This, together with a lack of obeying one of the basic rules of underwater photography, namely *reducing the volume of water between the camera lens and the subject to a minimum*, accounted for lots of very average and monochromic effects that ended up in the round file on the floor without even being afforded the benefit of any technical analysis.

My growing love of diving the British coast and its fascinating marine life encounters grew along with my disillusionment of my photographic capabilities. Fortunately for me, two terrestrial encounters came to my rescue. The first was by way of the, then, newly-formed Bristol Underwater Photography Group where I met experienced underwater photographers, such as founder members Gordon James FRPS and AV photographer Alan Mildren. Here, for the first time, I was

Opposite:
The sun penetrates a kelp gulley at St Abbs.

136

able to compare my results with others and obtain sound advice on successful procedures.

Within months of joining the group I also attended a Martin Edge underwater photography course on the south coast. Here I met a man whose ability and enthusiasm to pass on both technical and practical skills, matched my hunger to devour it. A year later I vividly remember discussing with Martin a list of my photographic ambitions that he had asked me to write down. His general advice was that it was all possible with dedication and he encouraged me to 'go with the flow'. Five years later the only outstanding item on that list was to produce a photographic publication of the UK's generous share of the world's marine wildlife.

As mentioned earlier, the vast majority of my work is exposed using manual control. By this I retain full control over the exposure of most of my images. I work on a principle of 'keeping it simple' both by way of compositional elements and reducing variables by the use of consistent film stock and shutter speeds. Any bracketing of exposure is controlled by stepped strobe to subject distances and their relative lighting angles. By working in this consistent manner I can allow more attention to my subject interaction, perhaps getting closer to achieve better camera angles and more contrasting or dramatic composition.

Manual strobe control also allows me to use two or three compatible Nikonos cameras fitted with two-pin sealock connections on any one dive. This opens up restrictions of lens choice, perhaps allowing wide-angle and macro 2-1 as required and of course it doubles the amount of film available. I work with the full range of Nikonos lenses including the little used 80mm amphibious lens, which is excellent when used in conjunction with the supplementary Nikonos close-up outfit to produce a 1-2 ratio image. My favourite Nikonos 15mm lenses is never left on the shore at any time that I am in the water. For ambient and balanced light work I retain a Sekonic light meter linked to a small lanyard in my stab jacket pocket.   A nudibranch scenic

Maintenance and care of all types of underwater photography equipment demands specially disciplined and clinical cleaning to all 'user' O rings and their seals, soaking of equipment in fresh water to help remove the potential build up of corroding salt crystals, and at least annual maintenance to all hidden O rings to camera or housing controls. Any serious underwater photographer should retain spare compatible cameras etc, and perhaps a philosophical view that one day the sea will eventually penetrate their equipment. It is therefore also important to have some sort of planned 'flood procedure' to ease the stress of such situations.

The success of much marine life photography is often based on building acceptance by the subject within its territory, this can often take a lot of precious time and patience in a cold environment with air sources quickly dwindling. Once acceptance has been gained you have to get to know your subject and any particular habits or movements that might create a more dramatic image. Recognising those moments is one thing, capturing them on film quite another. But by sharpening general skills on more static subjects you can eventually 'get it all together' at the right moment.

The rewards to be gained from this approach can be two-fold. On a dive spent with a single subject you will undoubtedly learn much about its habits and will exit your dive thrilled by the experience, plus you have the possible bonus of a timeless dramatic image taken during your interactions with it.

Night diving creates opportunities for underwater photographers to photograph nocturnal subjects not seen during the day. It also allows some opportunities to get carefully closer to less tolerant daytime subjects that might be sleeping or reluctant to swim blindly away. Being totally strobe reliant on exposure, a photographer has the opportunity to create some very dramatic close images with lovely contrasting black-water backgrounds.

A single featherstar on an anchor chain link

139

Publication, competition and slide show presentations are the underwater photographers' medium for exposure of their work to others. I certainly now judge my current levels of success by the gaps in my storage system. At this point we join with photographers at large and have to consider the risk element of treasured images being parted with for publication. Will they be delivered to and returned from the publishers safely? Will the printers treat your images with the same care that you took taking them? Should you consider expensive duplication of all the material that you send out? It really is a gamble!

Accepting it, I have tried to reduce the odds somewhat by investing in building my own high-quality slide duplicator to reduce the costs of duplicating a retained copy of all the prime images that I dispatch for publication. These also serve well for slide show presentation, avoiding the general wear and tear created affecting original work.

Finally a word of warning to would-be underwater photographers. You could be considering dabbling with a fascinating subject that is capable of changing your whole way of life. Eleven years ago I had no particular interest in our marine environment and did not even own a land camera. A year after I started diving, my partner Julie generously purchased my first and still much-treasured Nikonos V camera for Christmas. During 1995 I completed well over three hundred hours underwater, covering the British isles from extreme south to north and taking over eight thousand images in the process.

Grey seal

Acknowledgements

When underwater, photographers have to rely on personal skills and a high level of commitment to achieve their images. Prior to diving, this work demands a lot of planning, equipment servicing and general technical support and diving facility backup in sometimes very remote locations. This requires the assistance of many other people of various skills. I wish to extend special thanks to the following individuals and organisations that have supported me so admirably both during and prior to the location work to produce images for this publication.

The Channel Islands
The Jersey Tourism Board
Surf Dive 'n' Ski, St Helier
James Nagy and John
Alison and Jamie

The Scillies
International Helicopters
Mark Groves Dive Centre
Olive Fiddler
Joe Foxcroft

The Manacles
Porthkerris Dive Centre
The entire Ansalmi family
Gary Fox and Nikki
Alan Mildren and Chris Chandler

Falmouth
Andrew Sawyer Parker
Gordon James FRPS

Plymouth Sound
Fort Bovisand Dive Centre
Peter Sieniewicz
Kit Macalister
John Souness
Dave Peake

Torbay Area
Fastrak Diver Training
Richard Moncad
Kelvin Curtis
John Maclarene

Alan Mildren
Andy Hibbert

Chesil Beach, Portland
Andrew Sawyer Parker
Alan Mildren
Paul Glendell

Lundy Island
Warden Ema Parkes
Paul Gilliland
Philip Robertson
Marcus Heyes
Andy Hibbert
John Heath

St Abbs Marine Reserve
Lawson Woods
Alan Mildren
Andrew Sawyer Parker
Martin Edge
Paul Glendell
Steve Lewins

The Sound of Mull
Philip Robertson
Alan Mildren
Lochaline Dive Centre

The Summer Islands
Philip Robertson
Alan Mildren
Atlantic Diving Services

General advice and assistance

The Bristol Underwater Photography Group for their consistent support, encouragement and general assistance.

Current State Diving for technical support, air supplies and professional advice.

English Nature for their support of the project in general.

Martin Edge for helping me to germinate the seed that produced this publication and pointing me in the right directions many years ago.

'Aquatic Eikon', the underwater image library, for professional understanding and release of some of my stock images to complete a more comprehensive coverage for this publication.

David Knight for his general assistance in all technical matters relating to both underwater photography and laboratory processing.

David Bellamy and the Marine Conservation Society for the Foreword and their support of this publication (editorial and publishing).

To my partner Julie for my first treasured Nikonos V and supporting me in what has been a very long sacrificial road in pursuit of marine life encounters and images.

Diving photographer Chris Chandler

English Nature: Marine Conservation and You

*E*nglish Nature is pleased to have been able to support the making of this book, which helps to demonstrate the wealth and wonder of the marine wildlife and the places that they inhabit.

English Nature (formerly part of the Nature Conservation Council) is the statutory adviser to government on nature conservation in England. We promote, directly and through others, the conservation of England's wildlife and natural features including, of course, in the marine environment. Our work includes: the selection, establishment and management of national nature reserves and marine nature reserves; the identification and notification of sites of special scientific interest; the provision of advice and information about nature conservation; and the support and conduct of research relevant to these functions.

What does that mean in terms of our marine work? Essentially that we are involved in a wide range of work including: liaison with a variety or organisations and sea users from recreational bodies to voluntary groups to government departments; identifying marine sites of nature conservation interest; helping to meet our national and international conservation commitments; carrying out relevant research, survey and monitoring; and of course promoting an understanding and appreciation of our marine wildlife heritage (something already close to most divers' hearts and the theme of this book).

This work is carried out at a wide range of levels, for example, in the wider sea one of our aims is to encourage sustainable use by influencing others to develop a duty of care for nature conservation. This might include encouraging the use of technology to minimise pollution or effective regulation of commercial activities and development. Through our estuaries and sensitive marine areas initiatives we are involved in many voluntary projects to develop management for the protection of marine sites. We also encourage the voluntary approach in our support of the voluntary Marine Nature Reserves Programme, which has helped to establish more than ten such reserves around the coast of England, including some well known dive sites (Kimmeridge, The Scillies and north Devon). We are involved with legally designated sites from international, such as the recent proposed special areas of conservation, to national, such as the marine nature reserve at Lundy. The latter is particularly important to us as a place to develop ideas about managing designated sites, whether it be monitoring, education or interpretation.

Much of this work depends on and is about you as members of the public. As divers, however, you are also particularly important as one of the few groups that see our marine wildlife heritage at close hand and some of the damage and destruction being caused to it. You have a vital role to play in helping to ensure that we protect and cherish this heritage. Many divers already do so either through a general level of awareness or through specific projects. The latter might include providing underwater footage to make a video about Lundy Marine Nature Reserve for the public or other interpretative projects, taking part in volunteer sublittoral surveys, such as through Seasearch, helping with the work of voluntary marine nature reserve groups, or demonstrating the beauty of our underwater life.

We place great importance on encouraging such work and building on the already significant nature conservation awareness amongst divers. In this way we can all do our bit to ensure that we and future generations can continue to enjoy the wonderful marine wildlife and habitats of Britain so ably displayed in this book.

Our work on estuaries, the coast and marine environment is led and co-ordinated by the maritime team. For more information about us and our work you can write to the maritime team at English Nature, Northminster House, Peterborough, PE1 1UA, England.

Silhouetted seaweeds